DURHAM
CITY
New Discoveries

DURHAM
CITY
New Discoveries

Michael Richardson

DB
PUBLISHING

First published in Great Britain in 2010 by The Derby Books Publishing Company Limited, 3 The Parker Centre, Derby, DE21 4SZ

This paperback edition published in Great Britain in 2013 by DB Publishing, an imprint of JMD Media Ltd

ISBN 978-1-78091-343-8

Printed and bound in the UK by Copytech (UK) Ltd Peterborough

CONTENTS

FOREWORD

Durham City New Discoveries is the 14th of Michael Richardson's books of Durham photographs. The first was published in 1994, Durham, The People and The Place 1914–39 – I have them all. Consistently, and from the beginning his work has shown attention to detail, imagination, freshness of choice, an enthusiasm and delight in the history of his city. This, his latest, has over 470 previously unpublished photographs from his splendid Gilesgate Photographic Archive, with informative captions of a high standard. Michael's books are a remarkable achievement. He has brought together not only images of the well-known and little-changing sites, but also those of the everyday life of the trades, institutions and transport. Also covered are some of the associated colourful personalities. He provides context, revives memories, and encourages us to search further.

Durham City has developed and changed since I started here in the mid-1960s, and the age of the digital camera is upon us. We are grateful to the early photographers of a small city, with their careful setting-up and discriminating eye for historic record of the unusual.

The Peninsula, Cathedral and Castle provides a matrix of geographic, monastic and historic stabilitas; upon which the passing generations have reflected strong pride in their community. I heartily commend this book. Michael's work in the pages which follow will, I know, enthral us and enhance our delight in the social history of Durham City and surroundings.

Roger Norris 2010
Deputy Librarian: Durham Cathedral 1966–2002
Chair: Trustees: Durham City Freemen

INTRODUCTION

Durham City New Discoveries is a pictorial history of Durham and contains over 470 photographs and informative captions. A unique feature of this volume is that all the images have been discovered during the last two years. As you view the historic photographs, you will no doubt see Durham City in a different light. All walks of life are portrayed. Many will notice familiar faces, some will even find past and present family members.

In this fast-moving world we now live in, it is easy to forget about the way of life that our ancestors had. These photographs show the close-knit community that Durham City once had (and still has in some areas). There are people who made their mark on the city in various ways: in education, sport, business, the church and military service. A mixture of activities, which involved all levels of society, are covered, for example Durham City Horse Parade, Durham Regatta and the Durham Miners' Gala.

On the outskirts of the city we have many interesting villages that now lie within the city's boundary. Most are generally thought of as former pit villages; however, many of them have a long history that pre-dates the mines. St Helen's Church, Kelloe, displays a 12th-century cross, for example. Many more gems are there to be found, and the likelihood is that this book will inspire you to visit and explore.

I hope that, after you have perused the following pages, you will see the importance of saving and sharing these images in book form.

'Preserving and presenting the past for the future'.

Michael Richardson, 2010

ACKNOWLEDGEMENTS

So many people have donated and loaned photographs to the Gilesgate Archive that it is impossible to thank them all. Special thanks go to Mr George Billingham, Mr Frank Bilton, Mrs Jean Blackburn, Miss Ethel Brewster, Mr Chris Carman, Mr Brian Hall, Mr Ian Forsyth, Mr Peter Jefferies, Mr and Mrs D. Jones, Mr Peter Killian, Miss Dorothy M. Meade, Mr and Mrs R. Mechen, Mr George Robert Savage Nelson, Mr Roger Norris, Mr Harry Pounder, Mr John Pounder, Miss Emma Richardson, Mrs Norma Richardson, the late Mr Joe Robinson, Mr Tommy Rowntree, Miss Amanda Stobbs, Miss H.C. Webster, Mr David Williams and Mr W.H.L. Wood. Thanks also to Clayport Library (reference section), Durham Record Office, Palace Green Library, Dean and Chapter Library, Durham Heritage Centre and Museum, The History of Durham Project and The City of Durham Trust.

If any readers have new material, photographs, postcards, slides, negatives or information they should contact:

Gilesgate Archive
C/o Michael Richardson
128 Gilesgate
Durham
DH1 1QG
Email: gilesgatearchive@aol.com
Telephone: 0191 3841427

THE BUILT ENVIRONMENT

The Built Environment

Durham Cathedral and St Oswald's Church from Nine Tree Hill, 1880s. In December 1915 the University Estates Committee asked the tenant farmer to arrange for further planting on the hill to take the number of trees up to nine. This was done in 1916. Today only six trees remain.

The building of the railway viaduct between June–July 1855, taken from the grounds of the County Hospital. During this stage, a joiner named John Proctor, aged 26, unfortunately fell to his death. This was the only fatality during its construction. The stone building in the foreground is Bee's Cottage. Through the left arch the Bethel Chapel can be seen, beyond the central arch, is Avenue House.

The Cathedral and Waddington Street Church, taken from near Flass Vale, 1880s. The clean look of the church is due to the fact that it was only recently built, having been completed, April 1872. The building on the bottom right still survives and is now a public house, The King's Lodge Hotel, previously called The Rose Tree. A public footpath still runs along the south side of the property.

The viaduct from near Flass Vale, c.1914. The 11 arches of the viaduct are clearly visible. The large property on the left, Flass House, then belonged to Mr George H. Proctor, printer and stationer, of No. 8 Market Place. For many years it was the headquarters for the Durham branch of the Red Cross. The small white boxes in the corner of the field are beehives. On the extreme right is the gatehouse of the Durham Miners' Hall.

North Road from the top of the Railway Viaduct, 1890s. The row of houses, top left, is Tenter Terrace. On the right is the distinctive Bethel Chapel, opened 13 August 1854. At centre right is the domed tower of the first Durham Miners' Hall, opened 3 June 1876.

A view from the south side of the railway embankment showing Durham County Hospital, *c*.1908. On the left is the spire and roof top of the United Reform Church in Waddington Street. Behind the hospital is the Western Hill area. This fine frontage is now hidden by a 1930s extension.

Shafto's Cottage, North Road, *c*.1850. The occupant, Lancelot Shafto, had fought a bitter battle with the railway company, at one time chasing surveyors from his land with a blunderbuss. The thought of leaving his beloved cottage was too much to bear, and he took his own life. His inquest was held in the Angel Inn, Crossgate, by Coroner J.M. Favell. The cottage stood on the south side of the present railway viaduct. It was buried intact during the construction of the south end of the railway viaduct embankment.

Durham Market Place in the 1880s. The large gathering has possibly gathered around a religious speaker standing near the church corner. At centre-left is an open-top horse-drawn caravan with the words 'God is Love', and at centre-right is a Punch and Judy stand. Note the empty niche above the church door prior to the statue of St Nicholas arriving.

The Market Place, July 1869. The picture shows the second water pant, erected in 1863, the Londonderry statue, unveiled in 1861, the second St Nicholas's Church, consecrated in 1858, and the Town Hall, opened on 29 January 1851. (Taken by Thomas Heaviside.)

Crowds standing on and below Elvet Bridge, watching the river in flood, c.1921. On the right a lady is standing precariously on the lower balcony of Brown's boathouse, now a riverside bar.

The Londonderry statue in the Market Place, 1880s. Inscribed on the granite plaque are the words: CHARLES WILLIAM VANE STEWART / 3rd MARQUIS OF LONDONDERRY / 1st EARL VANE AND BARON STEWART / OF STEWARTS COURT K.G.G.C.B. / LORD LIEUTENANT COUNTY OF DURHAM / AND FOUNDER OF SEAHAM HARBOUR / GENERAL IN THE ARMY / BORN MAY 8th 1778 DIED MARCH 6th 1854. On 2 December 1861 the statue was unveiled in the presence of the Londonderry family, Benjamin Disraeli, the sculptor Raffaelle Monti, local dignitaries, staff of the North Durham Militia, the 2nd Durham Artillery and the 3rd and 7th Durham Rifles. The statue and plinth were moved several yards south in 2010, despite widespread public opposition.

One half of a stereo view, showing the castle, cathedral and Framwellgate Bridge, 31 July 1860. Note the dried-up state of the river bed and the steps leading from the yards in Back Silver Street.

Match-stick-like figures, skating on the frozen river near Framwellgate Bridge, 1900s. Because this stretch had a weir at each end, it was more likely to freeze over in bad winters, and it was a favourite spot for brave skaters. (Taken by W. Wilkinson.)

A faded view showing the west side of the castle, taken from a stereo photograph, 31 July 1860. On the left is a cottage, No. 22 South Street, with an attached wooden sign advertising William Herbert, gardener. Herbert lived there from 1854–80.

Looking across the river towards South Street from below the castle in the 1900s. On the right side of the slope are established walled gardens, one with a large glass-house.

The old St Margaret's Rectory at the head of South Street, 1900s. The fine, stone property, built *c.*1850, no longer serves that purpose. Now called St Margaret's House, it is the home of a canon of the cathedral.

The cathedral from St Margaret's churchyard, Crossgate, 1900s. This area is one of the oldest parts of Durham. In the early Middle Ages it was a separate borough, comprising of Crossgate, Allergate and South Street). It was under the lordship of Durham Priory and had its own borough court but had no market. Crossgate was first joined with the centre of Durham, where the markets were held, when Bishop Flambard built Framwellgate Bridge in about 1120.

South Street Mill and Durham School boathouse, 1900s. The name of the dog in the bottom-left corner was recorded on the reverse of the photograph. He was called 'Buzzer'. In October 1902 a pair of royal swans were given to the city from the Keeper of Swans on the instruction of the Lord Chamberlain. They arrived in Durham by train.

South Street Mill and house, c.1901. The picture shows the mill-race gates and two of the occupants, possibly the Newby family (later followed by the Rutherfords), one in the garden, and the other in the doorway. Note the hand-operated wooden mechanism for controlling the water flow for the mill. (Taken by W. Wilkinson.)

The Watergate, South Bailey, 1920s. The fine, elaborate door-head canopy of No. 12, now St Cuthbert's Society, is seen on the right. This was added by J.G. Wilson, who purchased the house about 1900. He had a similar hood made for his solicitors's office at No.5 North Bailey. On the reverse of the original postcard was written: 'A Sunday morning in Durham.'

Looking down the nave of St Mary le Bow Church, 1900s, showing the 17th and early 18th-century woodwork. The church is now Durham Heritage Centre and Museum. Many photographs from Gilesgate Archive are displayed here, along with a number of regularly changing exhibits relating to Durham City's rich social history. (Taken by W. Wilkinson.)

No. 12, The College (the area behind the cathedral), was once part of the Priory Guest Hall. It is of mediaeval origin and was rebuilt in the 17th century, with further alterations made in the 18th and early 19th centuries. This picture shows it during the 1920s. (Taken by R. Johnson and Son, Gateshead.)

The Deanery, showing Dean Henson's study and library, c.1914. With the use of a magnifying glass on the original postcard, a photographic portrait showing John Wilson, MP, Secretary of the Durham Miners' Association, can be seen on the mantelshelf.

The drawing room of The Deanery, situated in The College, behind the cathedral, c.1914. The postcard shows its 18th-century, hand-painted wallpaper, which still survives. Curiously it is believed not to have been put up before 1912 as it is not present on photographs taken for *The Story of the Deanery 1070–1912* by G.W. Kitchin.

The Deanery's sitting room, *c.*1914. At the time of this photograph it was lived in by Dean Hensley Henson. The postcard was published by A. Bailes, No. 50 Saddler Street.

The 17th-century Alms Houses, Palace Green, 1900s. It was founded in 1666 for four men and four women. On the left is part of Cosin's Hall; at the time of the postcard, the second window from the right had been converted into a door. Pictured on its right is a stone projection, which is a later addition, attached to the Alms Houses. This no longer survives.

The Last Supper panel, behind the High Altar in Durham Cathedral, 1860s. Carved from limestone by White of London, it was commissioned in 1849. This still survives in storage, hidden away in the upper triforium of the nave. (Taken by Thomas Heaviside.)

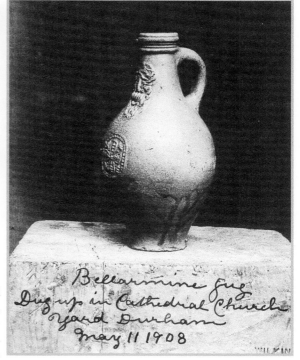

A bellarmine jug, which was dug up in the Cathedral churchyard on 11 May 1908. It was while Mr G. Burton, sub-verger and sexton, was digging a grave in the north-east portion of the churchyard, that he found the jug at a depth of six feet. It stood about eight inches high and was placed in the Chapter Library for safe-keeping. These jugs originated in the Germanic areas of Europe in the early 1500s. The location of this one today is uncertain. (Taken by W. Wilkinson.)

A member of the Cathedral clergy shows a young visitor around the Galilee Chapel for the first time in December 1939. The chapel dates from the late Norman period, c.1175–80, and was built by Bishop Hugh le Puiset. From 1370 it became the shrine of Saint Bede, and it was later used as the Consistory Court for the diocese. James Wyatt, the cathedral architect, wanted to demolish it, but fortunately he was stopped.

Divinity House annexed to the old Grammar School, Palace Green, 1900s. The property faces the north door of the cathedral and is now used by the university's music department. Between 1921–32 it was the residence of the cathedral librarian and author, Mr J. Meade Falkner. Note the wooden shutters on the ground-floor windows and flower boxes on the first floor. (Taken by W. Wilkinson.)

The ante-room of Durham Castle, 1900s. This room leads to the Bishop's suite. Through the open door in the right corner is seen the Black Staircase, which dates from the time of Bishop Cosin in 1662.

The west end of the Tunstall Chapel, Durham Castle, 1880s. The chapel was completed in 1545, and the east end altered by Bishop Cosin between 1660–72. This view shows the organ, which was officially opened on 1 May 1880. This was constructed by Harrison and Harrison using some of the former choir screen and parts of the old cathedral organ, which was replaced in 1876. It was restored in 1925 as a memorial to those students killed in World War One.

The fine, oak panelling in the room at the bottom of the Black Staircase, Durham Castle, in the 1900s. This carved woodwork once formed the organ-screen in the cathedral. It no longer survives in this location, and its whereabouts are now uncertain. (Taken by W. Wilkinson.)

The remains of one of the 13th-century semi-circular bastions of the old gaol in Saddler Street, 1900s. This one survives today, reached by a door leading to a passage on the right-hand side of the road, near the junction with Owengate. At the time of this postcard, the area was being used to store wood; note the handcart on the right.

Looking down into Millburngate from the junction of Crossgate and South Street, *c*.1905. On the extreme left is a barber's pole. Another one is seen outside the building further down on the right. The property with the corner window is the King William IV public house, with the original street name in the form of a stone tablet in the wall, which reads: 'King Street 1831'. On the far right is the Five Ways Inn, and below that is Burkett's, with a sign above the door, reading: 'The Original Italian Ice Cream', and, below it, A.T. Douglas, grocer. In the distance is the gable end of the Barley Sheaf Inn, No. 122 Millburngate, then run by J. Mutton. (Taken by W. Wilkinson.)

Looking down into Millburngate from Framwellgate, 1900s. On the left a group of young men pass the time away, some on their 'hunkers' (sitting on toes, with thighs resting on the calves of the legs, a manner of sitting peculiar to miners). Note the timber-framed gable of the building on the left. Unfortunately, Millburngate shopping centre and car park now occupy this whole area.

St Godric's Mission Room, Framwellgate, *c*.1900. The building on the right was part of Blagdon's Leather Works. Near the edge of that roof line is seen the spire of St Nicholas' Church, on the opposite side of the river, in the Market Place.

The Fram-Well, at the head of Framwellgate, 1850s. From 1450 the city's water supply was piped from a spring near this spot to an underground reservoir in the Market Place, which in turn fed the water pant. In the distance, on the left behind the well roof, is Kepier Hospital and, left of that, on the opposite side of the river, is Crook Hall. On the skyline to the right is a steam train leaving Gilesgate Goods Station.

Durham from Crook Hall Farm, 1900s. Note the quaint stream winding down towards the fence. The chimney on the right belonged to the old gas works in Sidegate and the one in the central area, on the other side of the river, to the carpet factory. This postcard was sent to Miss Beatie Hopps at Old Durham Farm from 'Sidney'.

An architect's drawing of the proposed St Cuthbert's Mission Rooms at the head of Framwellgate, *c.*1898. It was designed by Messrs Plummer and Burrell and built by Mr C.W. Gibson of Atherton Street. The estimated cost was about £700, and the foundation stone was laid on 24 October 1898 by Mrs Darwin of Dryburn Hall (great-niece of W.L. Wharton). It served the church until 1949, when it was sold and became a paint store. Later modernised and used as an office for a firm of landscape architects, it remains as an office today.

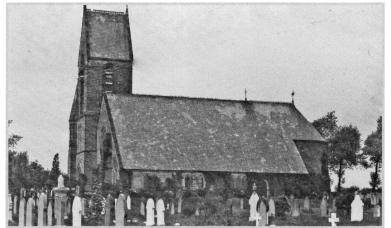

The south side of St Cuthbert's Church, North Road, 1909. The church was consecrated on 27 August 1863. It was designed by Edward R. Robson (1835–1917) and built using Penshaw sandstone, which unfortunately has worn very badly over the years. A community room was added to the north side in 1991. The churchyard has many interesting headstones that cover the city, as well as Framwellgate Moor and Brasside.

A section of the business area of North Road, *c.*1905. The central sign reads: 'Thorne's For Fishing Tackle', and one behind it reads 'Singers', advertising the sewing machines. On the extreme right was J.R. Burnet, optician and jeweller. These shops stood near to where Yates's Wine Lodge is now located. (Taken by W. Wilkinson.)

Repair work being carried out on the Obelisk, North Road, 1900s. It had been erected in 1850 by Mr W.L. Wharton of Dryburn Hall at his own expense. Its purpose was to mark true north for sighting the telescope belonging to the university observatory, situated at Potter's Bank. At the bottom-right is the tower of St Cuthbert's Church, North Road. (Taken by W. Wilkinson.)

North Road, showing the old bus station, 15 March 1953. The shop on the left was Porter's, the grocer, and next door was the Northern Electricity Board showrooms and office. (Taken by Frank Wilson.)

A busy North Road, 1900s. Showing the five ornate lamp stands on the left, near the four statues of the miners' leaders, situated on the frontage of the first Durham Miners' Hall, which opened 3 June 1876. The cart moving off in the centre has the name 'Moor Edge Laundry' on the rear doors. The skyline is dominated by the Victorian railway viaduct, officially opened 1 April 1857.

Durham Railway Station from the viaduct, *c.*1909. The south signal box no longer survives. On the right can be seen the ornate cast-iron canopy, regrettably removed in 1972, which matched that surviving on the northbound platform.

A steam engine with the number 61079 pulling south-bound out of Durham Railway Station, 1950s. The B1 Class loco, built by the North British Locomotive Company of Glasgow in 1946, was withdrawn from service in 1962 as British Rail converted to diesel engines. At the top of the photograph in the centre is the old pavilion in Wharton Park, now removed. (Taken by Billy Longstaff.)

The guns on the battery, Wharton Park, *c.*1905. Two old men admire the fine view of the city from this vantage point. These guns were removed during World War Two to be melted down for the war effort. (Taken by W. Wilkinson.)

The well-preserved lead statue of Neptune in Wharton Park, 1930s. He was removed from his third pant head in the Market Place in 1923 after the large domed structure that he adorned became a traffic hazard. He was first placed on a rockery at the park and later he had a stone plinth built. In 1969 an official of the City Trust, Mr Roger Norris, said: 'We feel the statue should be preserved'. After years of vandalism he was restored by the Trust in 1986 and eventually brought back to the Market Place in 1991. He anticipates a further short journey soon (2010).

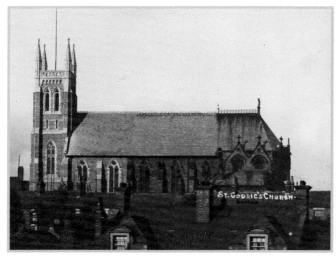

An unusual view of St Godric's Church from a roof-top in Neville Street, *c*.1910. Designed by E.W. Pugin, son of the more famous A.W.N. Pugin, it was officially opened on 15 November 1864. The *Durham County Advertiser* commented on the fact that those attending the ceremony were required to pay for admittance. Note the clean look of the new tower and west end extension, built between 1909–10. (Taken by W. Wilkinson.)

A postcard of the shrine of St Gerard Majella in St Godric's RC Church, Durham, *c*.1914. The Patron Saint of Motherhood was born in Muro, Italy, 6 April 1726 and died of tuberculosis, 16 October 1755, aged 29. The wall plaque is no longer at the church, and its present location is uncertain.

St Oswald's Institute, Church Street, 1900s. The land had previously been occupied by an old lodging house (see page 9). It was designed by Mr Love of Chester le Street, and the foundation stone was laid on 17 September 1902 by Dean Kitchin. Several years ago it was on the verge of being sold; fortunately it has now been given a new lease of life. (Taken by W. Wilkinson.)

A south-east view of St John's Church, Neville's Cross, Durham, 1900s, prior to the adding of the chancel in 1908, which was a memorial to the Revd George Sydney Ellam, who was killed on a motorcycle nearby on 13 May 1905. The church was consecrated on 8 April 1896.

Dene Head House, Ryton on Tyne, Gateshead, was built using reclaimed stone from the ancient St Nicholas's Church, Durham Market Place. The demolition of the church commenced, 21 May 1857. The stones around the windows, with a decorative chevron-zigzag pattern, were from the east end of the old chancel. This area had previously been altered and rebuilt in 1841 to widen the access from Claypath. The photograph dates from the 1920s.

The south aisle of St Margaret's Church, 1900s. Note the roller blinds to keep out the bright evening sun. The south arcade dates from about 1150. On the reverse of the photograph is the name 'H.S. Harrison'. He was of the organ makers family and worshipped here. It is likely that he also took this photograph.

The north aisle of St Margaret's Church, Crossgate, 1900s. Thought to have been constructed around 1195 by the same masons who worked on St Oswald's Church, Elvet. The Victorian stained-glass window at the west end of the aisle is dedicated to the memory of Francis Humble and the Revd R.W.L. Jones. The church celebrated its 850th anniversary in 2010.

An interior view of St Nicholas' Church, Market Place, 1900s. The pews were removed between 1980–81 when the church was reordered. It was officially reopened on 23 October 1981. Note the former font, matching pulpit and ornate gas chandeliers. The chancel arch is now partitioned, with the lower portion fitted with sliding glass doors, forming a quiet chapel.

St Nicholas' cemetery, near The Sands, c.1895. The picture shows the grave of Jane Hall, wife of William, landlord of the Grapes Inn, No. 16 Claypath. The iron-work was taken away for the war effort between 1939–45. The row of terraced houses to the right are the rear of those in Providence Row. (Taken by W. Wilkinson.)

The redundant brick kiln (Grade II listed) near Kepier Farm, 1930s. This was built by John Thwaites *c.*1860. 'Harper's Pond' stood nearby, created as part of the operations for digging clay for the brick works. It was dangerously deep and was filled in during the early 1960s.

The remains of the old stone arch belonging to Kepier Mill, early 1960s. The mill, which dated from the mediaeval period, stood opposite Kepier Hospital gateway. It was destroyed in a fire on 24 September 1870. Fragments of the millrace also survive. (Taken by Hilary Webster.)

The Market Place, 15 March 1953. The businesses, left to right, are: Lloyds Bank, Hepworth's, Donkins, Duoro Wine Shops Ltd., the office for the *Sunderland Echo*, Prudential Assurance Company and the Market Hotel. (Taken by Frank Wilson.)

The building of Millburngate Bridge, early 1960s. In the distance, on the left, are the properties in Claypath, demolished shortly after this photograph was taken to make way for the new bridge and underpass.

The ancient Paradise Lane, off Claypath, 22 March 1953, showing the well-trodden cobbled surface. The buildings in the distance are the backs of those on Elvet Bridge. By about this time the whole area was almost derelict. (Taken by Frank Wilson.)

The frontage of Ivy Cottage, c.1910. The occupant, Mrs Susannah Nelson, is standing in the decorative trellis canopy. She reached the grand age of 100 before her death in 1940. The building stood next to the grounds of Leazes House, (later occupied by Durham High School), near Brown's boathouse.

A postcard of the Durham Co-operative and Industrial Society Limited, Claypath, 1911. The inserts are the Neville's Cross branch (see page 47) at the top and, below it, three portraits of the founding members of the society. The card was produced for the Co-op's Jubilee, 1861–1911.

The Congregational Church, Claypath, *c.*1905. Left of the church is the original frontage of the Maltman Inn. Its neighbour on the left was the shop of William Wasey, saddler and harness maker. The latter was demolished in the late 1920s to make way for the frontage of the Palladium Cinema. The second building up from the church was then Durham City Working Mens' Club. (Taken by W. Wilkinson.)

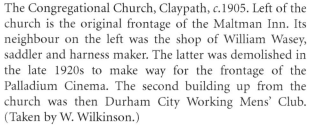

Mrs Burnip (on the reverse of the original is the name Jesse) with her Jack Russell dog outside No. 24 Gilesgate, *c.*1930. This house is situated to the right of the Woodman Inn, Gilesgate. These properties, along with many others in the locality, once belonged to the Gilligate Trust (Gilligate Church Estate Charity). Unfortunately, all but two of the houses were sold for a song not too many years ago.

No. 14a Gilesgate, *c.*1908. The frontage remains the same, apart from the wooden shutters. Almost all of the houses in this area would have had these fitted on the ground-floor windows. Many frames still have the hooks for the hinges. The postcard is signed on the reverse: 'From F.B.'

Bower Bank, the lane leading from behind St Giles's Church to St Hild's College, 12 April 1953. On the right is the rear of Grove House and the cathedral can be seen on the skyline. (Taken by Frank Wilson.)

The secluded frontage of Grove House, Gilesgate, 1900s. The building is situated behind St Giles's Church, and it can be reached by the steps behind the church or by a long driveway from the road on the south side of Gilesgate Bank. It was reputed by a number of former occupants to be haunted. The house, which is listed in the *Durham Directories* in the 1860s, has recently been converted into apartments. (Taken by George Fillingham.)

An early 19th-century engraving of St Giles's Church, Gilesgate. It shows the south porch and wall prior to the addition of the south aisle, which was added during the restoration between 1874–76. Some of the memorials survive and stand against the churchyard wall, behind the church.

The Norman Church of St Giles, Gilesgate, standing prominent on the south hillside of Gilesgate, 1900s. The church was founded in June 1112, and in 1143 it was fortified by the lawfully elected Bishop William of St Barbara, former Dean of York. He and his troops had chosen the building as a base and surrounded it with a rampart for defence. They were only here for a few days, leaving after a number of failed attempts, both forceful and peaceful, to take the seat from the unelected Bishop William Cumin. (Taken by John Edis.)

Houses at the top of Gilesgate Bank, on the south side, to the left of St Giles's Church drive, 1950s. The archway on the extreme left led to a yard (No. 149 Gilesgate), which was occupied by tenement properties. The house with the large shop window, No. 154 Gilesgate, was then a shared dwelling. In the late 1930s it had been a grocers, tea and provision merchants, run by Mrs Jane Smith. These old properties were demolished in the early 1960s to make way for council houses.

The 'Duck Pond' area (left), Gilesgate, late 1920s. This street is one of the ancient roads leading into the city and has more or less remained unchanged at this point. On the left are two of the three mock-Tudor houses that were built around the 1900s. The pond area would have been a long-established meeting place for the inhabitants as far back as mediaeval times. An air-raid shelter and water tank were located here during World War Two and were removed c.1946.

GILESGATE

An aerial view of Wood and Watson's 'pop' factory, early 1950s. The building on the right is the former nursery school, erected during World War Two. In the top-left corner is the 'Duck Pond' area. St Giles's cemeteries can be seen, the one in the bottom left having opened in 1927, and the one in the right corner opened in 1870. The factory and school site are now occupied by houses and apartments called St Giles's Close.

Durham from Pelaw Wood, 1880s, showing the old footbridge crossing Pelaw Wood beck. In November 1917 Lord Londonderry, the owner of the wood, was forced to sell off some of his outlying properties due to heavy death duties and taxes. Knowing the great value the citizens placed upon this wood, he decided to gift it to the city and wished it to be associated with the memory of the brave Durham soldiers who were sacrificing their lives in World War One.

The newly built concrete retaining wall below Pelaw Wood, 1938. Prior to the wall being constructed, the lower path was almost washed away by erosion due to flooding. The footpath would lead you to Old Durham Gardens, situated at the east end of the wood.

The modernisation of the old swimming baths, Old Elvet, 1961. The building and surrounding land is now set to be redeveloped for housing, despite public opposition. It is a missed opportunity for creating a new city park.

The Revd Grimshaw Yates (born Oswaldtwistle, Lancashire) in the pulpit of the Methodist Chapel, Chapel Passage, Old Elvet, 1900s. Note the box pews. This building was later used by the Salvation before they moved to Saddler Street.

The white-washed vennel (a northern name for a passageway between properties) between Nos. 29 and 30, running from the back lane near The Racecourse to the top of Old Elvet, 1950s. The brick archway no longer survives. (Taken by Frank Wilson.)

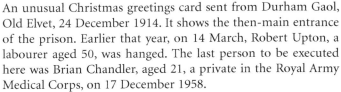

An unusual Christmas greetings card sent from Durham Gaol, Old Elvet, 24 December 1914. It shows the then-main entrance of the prison. Earlier that year, on 14 March, Robert Upton, a labourer aged 50, was hanged. The last person to be executed here was Brian Chandler, aged 21, a private in the Royal Army Medical Corps, on 17 December 1958.

The 17th-century staircase situated in The Royal County Hotel, Old Elvet, 1950s. The premises were renovated by F.W. Goodyear and Son, Durham, in 1925–26. This fine oak staircase with elm panels was installed by Bowman and Son of Stamford. It is said to date from the Stuart period, *c.*1680, and had been taken from the demolished Stoughton Grange, Leicestershire.

A faded postcard, thought to be Mrs Taylor, left, and an assistant, near her fishmonger's shop at No. 1 Church Street, *c.*1903. The premises stood near the forked junction at the lower end of Church Street.

The Victorian hand-operated fire appliance belonging to Durham Gaol, late 1920s. The photograph was taken in 'B' wing and shows the wire netting between the upper galleries, erected to prevent suicide attempts.

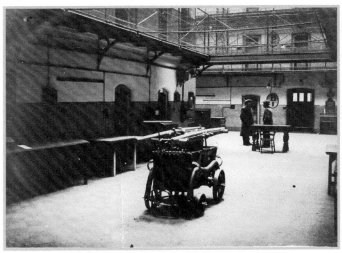

Looking up towards New Elvet from the bottom end of Elvet Bridge, 15 March 1953. The Georgian properties on the left were unlawfully demolished in 1975. They had to be rebuilt to more or less the exact replica of what had been taken down. Note the fine road surface, consisting of granite setts. (Taken by Frank Wilson.)

The interior of an unknown Durham church, 1860s. The pointing on the chancel walls suggests a recent restoration or even a rebuild. To the left of the chancel is an organ chamber. (Taken by Thomas Heaviside.)

The stone-built Low Dryburn Cottage, North End, 1950s. It was taken down when the new road, known as Southfield Way, was built, leading up towards the Lanchester Road from Durham County Hall roundabout. (Taken by Desmond Kelly.)

The entrance to Mavin Street, 22 March 1953. The street was named after the builder, George Mavin, No. 32 Gilesgate and was situated off Hallgarth Street. The car looks like an Austin Seven from the 1930s. The cobbled surface has since become an eyesore due to the fact that it is a private road. (Taken by Frank Wilson.)

Aden Cottage, Long Garth, Whitesmocks, Crossgate Moor, 1950s. At the time of this photograph it was the home of the Bradford family. Although called a cottage, it is a large dwelling surrounded by trees, with its own tennis court, and is reached by road from the A167, south of St Nicholas Drive.

Croftonholme, Crossgate Moor, *c.*1907. At the time of the postcard it was lived in by Mr Crofton Maynard, solicitor, and coroner for the Easington ward. Born in the North Bailey, he was the son of Thomas C. Maynard, coroner, attorney and solicitor of Holywell Hall, Brancepeth. Croftonholme was renamed Fernhill around 1915–19. It is situated on the A167, Newcastle Road, secluded high on the left along a dirt track called Club Lane, south of Whitesmocks Avenue.

Croftonholm, Durham.

Western Lodge, Whitesmocks, 1900s. Built in the early 19th century, it incorporated the remains of an earlier 18th-century building, which was originally a coaching inn called Whitesmocks Inn. This is the origin of the name now given to the area. The property is now split into two separate dwellings, Western Lodge and Grey Lodge. In recent years Dr Robert Catty formerly of Claypath Medical Practice lived in one half.

An architectural drawing by G.M. Kitchen of Observatory House, Potters Bank, taken from *The Building News*, 18 January 1901 (although the house was there in 1898). It was built for Professor R.A. Sampson, MA, and is located to the left of the entrance to the observatory.

The construction of the new A167 road bridge across the main railway line, Crossgate Moor, 17 August 1952. Note the old stone bridge behind. (Taken by Frank Wilson.)

Neville's Cross branch of the Durham Co-operative Society, 1911. This was Durham's first branch and had opened on 12 April 1909. It stood near the present traffic-lights at Neville's Cross, now demolished to make way for an extension to the nearby industrial laundry. On the extreme left is the former Neville's Cross Primitive Methodist Chapel.

The old Darlington to Newcastle Road, showing Cottage Row, Neville's Cross, 2 December 1951. The old houses on the right were removed to make way for the new road. The large building on the left, in the distance, is the Neville's Cross Co-operative Store. (Taken by Frank Wilson.)

Neville's Cross Inn, *c.*1906, viewed from Neville's Cross Bank. The landlord was then J. Hedley. Traffic for Newcastle turned left along St John's Road, crossing the railway cutting by a stone bridge that has since been demolished (see page 47). The postcard had been sent to Mrs J. Willis, The Poplars, Shincliffe Bank Top.

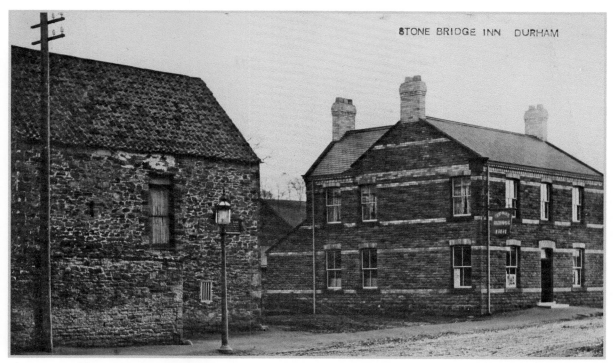

The Stone Bridge Inn, 1900s, situated on the left hand side of the road as you leave Neville's Cross Bank towards Langley Moor. The old barn on the left was later demolished, and a modern house now occupies the site.

An engraving of the Revd John Sudbury, Dean of Durham 1662–84, a close friend of Bishop John Cosin. After the Restoration of the Monarchy he founded a library in the former monastic refectory, and by 1676 it contained around 1,000 books. Today it is part of the Dean and Chapter collection.

A sketch of Tommy Sly of Durham from *c.*1810. A well-known eccentric character in the city, he had been a resident of the poor house for many years. He was a familiar sight, with his coat of many colours and side-drum, especially on public occasions when his services could be hired out to the highest bidder. He is seen in the Market Place next to the pant.

The Revd Henry Philpotts (1778–1869), vicar of St Margaret's Church (1810–20), Crossgate. One of 23 children, he was educated at Gloucester Cathedral School and elected a scholar of Corpus Christi College, Oxford, at the age of 13. His father was John Philpotts, factory owner, innkeeper, auctioneer and land agent to the Dean and Chapter of Gloucester. For 20 years Philpotts was chaplain to the Bishop of Durham, The Hon Shute Barrington. He later became Bishop of Exeter in 1830. He founded the theological college at Exeter and spent large sums on the restoration of the cathedral there. In 1833 he was apparently paid £13,000 in compensation when the slaves who had formerly belonged to the Society for the Propagation of the Gospel were emancipated.

The Hon Rt Revd Henry Montague Villiers, Bishop of Durham (1860–61). Educated at Christ Church, Oxford, he was the grandson of the 1st Earl of Clarendon. *Punch* ran a cartoon of him on 9 March 1861 in relation to the 'Durham Cheese Affair'. He had appointed Edward Cheese, his son-in-law and domestic chaplain, to the lucrative living of Haughton le Skerne, near Darlington. The *Manchester Guardian* newspaper accused him of gross nepotism and he became a target of wounding criticism. He died on 9 August 1861 and is buried in the chapel at Auckland Chapel.

Mr Richard Lawrence Pemberton of Hawthorn Tower, 1860s. Pemberton was born 1832 and lived at Bainbridge-Holme, Sunderland and Belmont Hall (now Ramside Hall, later occupied by his son, Dr John Stapylton Grey Pemberton). His father, also called Richard, was a colliery owner and died in 1843, making Richard an heir at the age of 12. He started his education at Houghton Grammar School before continuing to Eton and then Oxford. In the early 1850s Pemberton gave away the land on which Belmont Church was built. He died 21 June 1901, aged 69, and is buried in the family plot in Hawthorn village churchyard.

A portrait printed on silk of Mr John Bright, Esq, Member of Parliament for Durham City from July 1843–47. Born in 1811, he was the son of Jacob Bright of Greenbank, near Rochdale. He was a Quaker by faith and a Radical in politics. While MP for Durham, Bright was famous as one of the leaders of the successful campaign for the repeal of the corn laws, which kept the cost of food artificially high. After Durham he became MP for Manchester between 1847–57 and then Birmingham until his death on 27 March 1888.

The Rt Revd C.T. Longley (1794–1868), Bishop of Durham. Longley was educated at Westminster School and Oxford. He became an ordained deacon in 1818 and a priest in 1819, his first appointment being curate of Cowley, Oxford. He became the vicar of the parish in 1823. Later, in 1829, he was invited to become headmaster at Harrow School. In 1836 Longley was appointed Bishop of Ripon then, on 13 October 1856, Bishop of Durham. He went from Durham to be Archbishop of York in 1860 and in 1862 became Archbishop of Canterbury. He died on 27 October 1868.

Lt Edward Duncombe Shafto, RA, 1860s. He was the eldest son of the Revd A. Shafto and Dorothea (née Wilkinson). Promoted to captain, Shafto was gazetted to the Royal Artillery in 1861 and went to India in 1870 as Adjutant to the 16th Brigade RA. He was killed during the second Anglo-Afghan War (1879–80), when the magazine in the ancient fortress of Bala Hissar, Kabul, exploded on 14 October 1879. (Taken by Thomas Heaviside)

An unknown Durham character with his churchwarden's pipe, top hat and newspaper, 1860s. The photograph was taken by J. Kirkley, Paradise Gardens (near Elvet Bridge). This photographer's images are quite scarce.

Mr James Anderson, nurseryman, of Pelaw Terrace, Gilesgate, 1860s. A native of Banff in Scotland, Anderson had resided in Durham for about 30 years. He was the proprietor of the Wear Nurseries until his death on 30 October 1868, aged 49.

Lord Boyne (28 May 1830–30 December 1907), Gustavus Russell Hamilton-Russell, eighth Viscount of Brancepeth Castle, c.1864. He married the Hon Katherine Scott, third daughter of John, second Earl of Eldon, and had 12 children. He died on 30 December 1907 at Burwarton Hall, Bridgnorth, Shropshire. He was buried in the family vault in St Brandon's Churchyard, Brancepeth Village.

Lady Boyne (15 December 1837–19 May 1903), Katherine Frances, c.1864, with baby Gustavus William Hamilton-Russell. Katherine died at Brancepeth Castle and is buried in the family vault. (Taken by Thomas Heaviside.)

Mr George Greenwell, JP, *c*.1880. He was the third son of Mr John Greenwell of Red Barnes, near Bishop Auckland, and the founder of the well-known Durham establishment of Greenwell's, a grocer, tea dealer, wine and spirit merchant, Albert House, No. 33 Silver Street. He had served his apprenticeship with J.R. Chapman, grocer and tea dealer, No. 16 Market Place. He was also an old member of the Norman and Marquess of Granby Lodges of Freemasons. He died on 14 November 1890 and is buried in a brick-lined grave in St Cuthbert's Churchyard, North Road. (Taken by R. Herbert, No. 3 Silver Street.)

The Revd Canon George Body, doctor of divinity, preacher, writer and social reformer, in the 1880s. He came to Durham in 1885 to take up the work of Canon Missioner in the Diocese, with a salary of £1,000 a year. He was the author of several theological books. He died on 5 June 1911, aged 72, and is buried to the left of the north door in the cathedral churchyard (see page 110).

Mrs Christiana Heawood (Chrissie Tristram) and daughter Emily, 41, Old Elvet, 1891. She was born at Castle Eden, the sixth daughter of Canon Henry Tristram and wife of mathematics professor Percy John Heawood. He was the Vice-Chancellor for the University of Durham between 1926–28. The last seven years of her life was spent at No. 11 South Bailey, she died on 24 July 1954, aged 95. (Taken by F.W. Morgan.)

Lt Col George Francis White, DL (1808–98), Chief Constable of Durham from 7 November 1848 until his retirement, 31 March 1892. Prior to his appointment he was an army major, second in command of the 31st Regiment, and had served during the First Sikh War in 1845–46. Upon taking the command of the Durham Force, he reorganised it and introduced a new code of regulations. He died on 23 July 1898.

Councillor Henry Edwin Ferens, MA, a solicitor of No. 89 Gilesgate, 1890s. Born Gilesgate in 1864, Ferens was educated at Richmond School and the University of Durham. He was a keen rugby player and later played for the city. He was the father of Cecil Ferens (see page 80) and founded the well-known solicitors Ferens and Son. He died on 16 June 1933.

Councillor William Thwaites in 1901. Thwaites was a shoe and boot maker from No. 26 New Elvet. He became a Wesleyan Methodist preacher at the age of 18, serving 43 years on the Durham circuit. He died on 1 April 1902, aged 62, and is buried in St Oswald's cemetery. His son, Thomas, was killed in action at Ladysmith, South Africa, on 12 January 1900, aged 27.

An unidentified nun, 1890s, possibly one of the newly appointed teachers at St Godric's School, Castle Chare, which had opened in October 1898. (Taken by W. Wilkinson.)

Mr Henry Collins, an ex-miner of No. 26 Garden Street, Houghall, 26 November 1897. Collins was known as 'The Royal Pitman' (see page 114). He died on 18 May 1908, aged 78, at No. 30 Newcastle Street, Brandon Colliery. His family memorial in St Mary's Churchyard, Shincliffe, records the tragic losses he had suffered: his son, Thomas Henry, drowned in the River Wear near Shincliffe on 21 October 1860, aged 4½ (his body was found near Chester le Street on 23 January 1861); his wife, Isabella, died on 7 November 1874, aged 42; his daughter Elizabeth Ann, died on 12 November 1874, aged 12; a second son, Thomas Henry, died on 12 November 1874, aged 14; another son, William, drowned in Houghall Pit Pond on 20 June 1874, aged 5; his son, Henry, died on 13 December 1874, aged 18 months; and a second daughter called Isabella died on 14 June 1876, aged 4. (Taken by John Edis.)

The Revd Arthur Watts, Vice Principal of Bede College, *c.*1900s. Born in Northampton on 23 October 1838, Watts attended Cheltenham Training College in 1858 and qualified as a teacher. He came to Bede as a third tutor in 1871, and in 1874 he took the licence in theology and became an ordained deacon the following year and priest a year after that. In 1881 he became curate at St Mary's Church, Shincliffe, and eight years later he moved to St Michael's Church, Witton Gilbert. He died on 8 September 1933 and is buried at Witton Gilbert.

Councillor William H. Wood with his wife, Annie (née Watson) and children, Joseph Watson, Sidney and William, in front of The Laurels, Sherburn Road Ends, *c.*1907. Wood was founder of the City Mineral Water Works, Gilesgate, later called Wood and Watson Ltd (see page 40). He was elected Mayor of Durham in 1909 and 1919. He died on 22 February 1924 and is buried at St Giles's 1870 churchyard. (Taken by John Edis.)

The Rt Revd Bishop Alfred Robert Tucker in his study, *c.*1912. Born in 1849, Tucker grew up in the Lake District and followed in the footsteps of his family as an artist. He became a mature student at Oxford and was ordained at Bristol in 1882. His next move was as curate of St Nicholas' Church, Durham. When leaving Durham for Africa, parishioners and friends presented him with a gift of 150 gold sovereigns. In 1890 he was sent out by the Church Missionary Society to become the third Bishop of Eastern Equatorial Africa. Of the two previous bishops, James Hanington was murdered by natives in October 1885 and the other, Henry P. Parker, died of a fever in March 1888.

In 1897 Bishop Tucker was appointed the first Bishop of Uganda. After a total of 21 years in Africa he returned to Durham as a Residentiary Canon on 27 August 1911. He died in Westminster Deanery (with *The Times* newspaper on his lap)while on a visit to London on 16 June 1914. His grave is marked by a tall cross at the west end of Durham Cathedral Churchyard. (Taken by W. Wilkinson.)

Mr Harry (Henry) Marshall Imrie, 1877–1938. Born in Durham and educated at the Model School, Gilesgate, Imrie served his articles in mining at Littletown Colliery. He was a top player of Durham City Rugby Club and an English international. He held the record for the number of county caps won, with a total of 51, and also played against New Zealand in 1906. For 25 years he was under-manager at Langley Park Colliery. He then served 15 years as manager at Garesfield Colliery and, finally, spent 15 years at Chopwell Colliery where he was agent as well as manager. In retirement he moved to the family home at No. 22 Albert Street, Western Hill, with his sister, Miss Isabella Imrie. He died on 19 October 1938 and is buried in St Cuthbert's Cemetery, North Road.

Mr William Lax of South Street, father of Cuthbert (see below), *c.*1908. A retired shoe-maker, Lax died on 22 November 1909, aged 76, after a fire at his room in a tenement property at No. 10 South Street (he had previously lived at No. 13). He had been sharing a rear room with an old friend, William Chaytor Marshall, aged 79. Both died as a result of the fire, which was believed to have started when one of them was smoking in bed.

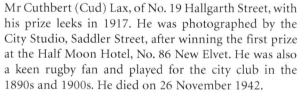

Mr Cuthbert (Cud) Lax, of No. 19 Hallgarth Street, with his prize leeks in 1917. He was photographed by the City Studio, Saddler Street, after winning the first prize at the Half Moon Hotel, No. 86 New Elvet. He was also a keen rugby fan and played for the city club in the 1890s and 1900s. He died on 26 November 1942.

County Councillor Alderman J. Lund, JP, 1900s. He began work in the mines at the age of 9½. After the Child Labour Act was passed he returned to Ludworth School and remained there until he was 12. He then became an apprentice gardener to Mr W.J. Herbert, Potters Bank. After that he returned to the pit, working at Framwellgate Colliery. He married Miss Lax of Elvet in 1880. In 1885 he was chosen by the miners to be their checkweighman and held this post until the pit closed in 1926. In 1895 he entered local politics and became a member of Durham Rural District Council. He was elected to represent the Elvet ward on Durham County Council in 1912 and was made an Alderman in 1921. He died on 25 August 1947, aged 90.

Alderman John Brownless, JP, with his wife Alice (who was nine years older) and daughter Rachel, at the front door of The Garth, South Road, *c.*1910. Brownless was born in Gilesgate in 1862, the eldest son of John Brownless of Whorlton Grange and formerly Belmont Hall. He was educated at the Model School, Gilesgate, then at a boarding school in the south, returning to complete his education at Durham School. He became an apprentice to Mr Maddison, a solicitor of Saddler Street, and in 1886 was admitted as solicitor, starting his own business a year later. He married Miss Wetheral, daughter of Mr H. Wetheral of the Bailey. He was elected a city councillor for the north ward in 1897 and was made an Alderman *c.*1903 and Mayor in 1908. Brownless died while on holiday in Scarborough on 4 September 1916. (Taken by W. Wilkinson)

Alderman Arthur Pattison, of No. 3 Ravensworth Terrace, Mayor of Durham, *c.*1906. He was born in the city and was a cathedral chorister from 1873–78, later attending Wolverley Grammar School, Worcestershire. He ran the well-known upholstery business on Elvet Bridge, which he had inherited from his aunt, Mrs M. Pattison. He was Mayor three times, in 1905, 1906 and 1917, as well as being a valued member of St Giles's Choir (see page 168). He died on 16 June 1926 and was buried in St Nicholas' Cemetery. (Taken by W. Wilkinson.)

The Revd Canon Professor Dawson Dawson-Walker, *c.*1920. Born on 20 December 1869 at Bradford, Dawson-Walker attended the grammar school there before gaining a Classical Scholarship at Corpus Christi, Oxford. Ordained in 1893, he became a curate in Bradford, leaving after one year to take up a Classics Lectureship at Durham University. After five years he became a theological tutor and in 1912 was appointed principal of St John's College. He resigned as principal in 1919 after being offered the appointments of canon residentiary of Durham Cathedral and university professor of divinity. He was also chaplain to the Corporation of Durham. Dawson-Walker was the author of a number of books, including *The Gift of Tongues* (1906) and was co-editor of *The Churchman* between 1910–14. He died on 28 January 1934.

Mr William Hopson Armstrong, piano dealer, 1900s. Armstrong had a music shop at No. 68 North Road and supplied, on credit terms, many brass instruments to miners' bands in the pit villages. He then lived in The Avenue, and his youngest son, W.A. Armstrong, was founder of the City Motor Engineers, Fowler and Armstrong Ltd. William Hopson Armstrong died aged 59 at his residence, No. 60 Hallgarth Street, on 31 January 1922.

Canon of Durham : Censor V. of St Mary - le - Bow

Vincent K Cooper.

The Revd Canon Vincent King Cooper of No. 16 South Bailey, rector of St Mary le Bow, North Bailey, *c.*1910. He graduated from Oxford in 1873 before being ordained as a deacon in 1874 and as a priest the following year. His first teaching post was assistant master at Bradfield College, then in 1875 he became headmaster at St Michael's College, Tenbury. He arrived in Durham the following year as minor canon and held a curacy at St Oswald's Church. He was later appointed sacrist and in 1887 precentor. In 1910 he became rector of St Mary le Bow and a rural dean. He was the author of *Tales from Euripides* (1879), a book about Greek mythology, which was reprinted in 2010. He died on 18 May 1922, aged 73, and is buried in Bow Cemetery, Potters Bank. (Taken by W. Wilkinson.)

Drawn by George Be...

The Revd Cyril Argentine Alington, drawn by George Belcher, *c.*1927. Born in Ipswich, the second son of the Revd Henry Giles Alington, an inspector of schools, Alington became headmaster of Eton College from January 1917–33 and also served as chaplain to King George V from 1921–23. He retired aged 60 in 1933 and came to serve as Dean of Durham until 1951. He founded The Friends of Durham Cathedral in 1933. In 1949 he received the Freedom of the City. Alington wrote hymns and was the author of over 50 books. His son, Patrick, a captain in the Grenadier Guards, was killed on 24 September 1943, at Salerno, Italy. Revd Alington died on 16 May 1955 at his home in Herefordshire and was buried in the north transept of Durham Cathedral.

Miss Eleanor C. Christopher, the first woman principal of St Hild's College (appointed 1910, retired Easter 1933), and her dog, 'Ting', *c.*1924. The daughter of a naval officer, Henry Seton Christopher, JP, she was born in Canada, spending most of her early years in the Isle of Man, where her father became bursar of King William's College. Christopher had studied in France and Germany, taking honours in modern languages at Oxford. Her first teaching post was in Liverpool. She later moved on to become headmistress of Leamington High School prior to her coming to Durham. She died on 18 February 1959, aged 85.

Mr George Henry Camsell (1902–66) in the 1920s. Born in Framwellgate Moor, Camsell started work as a coal-miner. One day he had a premonition of danger, and seconds later a heavy fall of stone killed his pony. After this experience he no longer wanted a life underground. He first played football in local village teams before going to Durham City Football Club in 1921. In 1925 he was transferred to Middlesbrough in settlement of a large debt by Durham. He won nine caps for England, scoring in every match he played. Between 1925 and his last game in 1939 he scored 345 goals in 453 games for Middlesbrough. After World War Two he joined the club's coaching staff. Camsell Court, Framwellgate Moor, was named in his honour in 2007, he died in March 1966. (Taken from a cigarette card.)

Men of the 2nd Durham Artillery Volunteers (17th Detachment) in Shoeburyness Camp, Essex, in 1888. Back row, left to right: Gnr Brass, Gnr Preece, Gnr Symes, Cpl Hedley, Bdr Kelly, Sgt-Major Lumsden and Bdr Lund. Front row, left to right: Sgt-Major Hopper, Sgt Maguire and Sgt Noble.

Soldiers from the 8th Battalion, Durham Light Infantry, at their annual camp in Rothbury, Northumberland, on 23–30 July 1910. (Taken by Speedy Photo Co., Durham.)

A group photograph of C Company of Durham University Officer Training Corps (OTC), taken at annual camp in Scarborough, 19 November 1912.

Major John Willan, JP, farmer of Shincliffe Croft (now called Corner House), Shincliffe, 17 August 1912. Willan was the son of James Willan, chemist of The Mount, Gilesgate. He had joined the Northumberland Yeomanry as a trooper in 1874 and was promoted to corporal in 1880. After a spell out he returned as quarter-master in 1892 and Hon Lieut of the 8th Durham Light Infantry. By March 1902 he was Hon Capt and in 1908 became Hon Major. He died on 1 August 1918, aged 69, and is buried in St Mary's Churchyard, Shincliffe.

The band of the 8th Battalion, Durham Light Infantry, identified by details painted on the base drum, wearing the latest webbing belts, *c.*1914. On 3 August 1914 (the day before Britain declared war on Germany) they were recalled back to Durham from annual camp in North Wales, to guard the coast at Whitburn. In April 1915 they were sent overseas as part of the 50th Division. (Taken by Speedy Photo Co., Durham.)

Soldiers of the 16th Battalion, Durham Light Infantry, photographed outside the Big Jug, Claypath, *c.*1915. The troops were billeted in the Bluecoat School, which was located behind the shops on the left of the public house. On 17 February 1915 nearly 200 men from A and B companies of the 16th DLI were invited to supper and entertainment in the lecture hall at the Wesleyan Church, Old Elvet. (Taken by Speedy Photo Co., Durham.)

Second Lieut Joseph Landt Mawson, Army Service Corps, c.1917. He saw service between 1917–19 as a heavy lorry driver and column officer of the 90 SBAC in France and Belgium. His home address was then No. 10 Ravensworth Terrace, Gilesgate. He spent some time as a motorcycle dispatch-rider and later suffered from shell-shock. After the war he joined his father's solicitor's practice, J. Mawson and Son. For many years he was clerk to Durham City Magistrates and solicitor to the university. He later moved to Shincliffe in 1924, where he died on 19 March 1976.

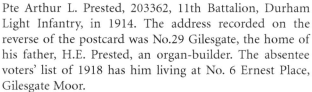

Pte Arthur L. Prested, 203362, 11th Battalion, Durham Light Infantry, in 1914. The address recorded on the reverse of the postcard was No.29 Gilesgate, the home of his father, H.E. Prested, an organ-builder. The absentee voters' list of 1918 has him living at No. 6 Ernest Place, Gilesgate Moor.

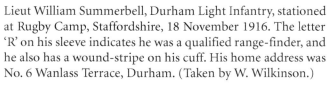

Lieut William Summerbell, Durham Light Infantry, stationed at Rugby Camp, Staffordshire, 18 November 1916. The letter 'R' on his sleeve indicates he was a qualified range-finder, and he also has a wound-stripe on his cuff. His home address was No. 6 Wanlass Terrace, Durham. (Taken by W. Wilkinson.)

Durham Light Infantry Regimental Police, billeted at Bluecoat School, photographed outside the boys' entrance (see page 147), *c*.1915. The school was vacated in November 1914 for the newly raised 16th Battalion, Durham Light Infantry (see page 67), with the children moved across the road to the Congregational Church. Note the handcuffs, and two of the men have 'RP' on their sleeves. (Taken by Speedy Photo Co., Durham.)

Gnr William Wright, 760868, Royal Field Artillery, *c*.1918. His home address was then No. 10 Douglas Villas, Gilesgate. He is photographed with his wife, Mary Emily Susan, and children, William Jnr, Lillian (Lily) and baby Joseph. In September 1918, his officer Capt. Cecil Jones RFA, was wounded by machine gun fire. With three others, Gunner Wright helped carry him from the trenches to a dressing station. An appeal was made in 1932 and in June of that year, Capt. Jones, a jeweller in Southend traced two of the men, Edmund Elliot of Silksworth and William Wright. He presented them with a handsome gold watch bearing the inscription: 'B.E.F. September 1918 – For Services Rendered'.

Sgt William Henry Smith, 22611, 13th Battalion, Durham Light Infantry, in 1916, aged 35. He was awarded his Military Medal for action on 10 July 1916 near Contalmaison on The Somme, France. Two men of the 12th DLI had been wounded by machine-gun fire and lay in the middle of a road. 'Sergeant Smith left his dug-out and dragged one of them, who had his thigh smashed, into the dug-out and applied a tourniquet. He then again left the dug-out and carried in the second man to a dressing station nearby. On both occasions Sergeant Smith was under fire.' This was the second time Smith had been mentioned in despatches. Prior to the war he was employed at Blagdon's Leather Works, No. 115 Framwellgate, and lived at New Elvet.

Pte T.W. Salkeld, 4/5 Battalion, Black Watch, *c.*1917. The photograph was taken at Longford Hall Hospital, Stretford, Manchester. His home address was No. 173 Gilesgate, the last house on the south side at the bottom of Gilesgate Bank. He died on 16 June 1976.

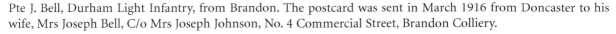

Pte J. Bell, Durham Light Infantry, from Brandon. The postcard was sent in March 1916 from Doncaster to his wife, Mrs Joseph Bell, C/o Mrs Joseph Johnson, No. 4 Commercial Street, Brandon Colliery.

Pte Matthew (Matty) Bunting, 83001/4435978, 2nd Battalion, Durham Light Infantry (1919–21). Born on 3 June 1900 in North Blyth, Northumberland, he moved to No. 7 Booth Cottages, West Sherburn, as a youth. Bunting had seen service in Russia after World War One. He spent a good half of his married life living in Annand Road, Gilesgate. He worked as a coal miner at Sacriston Pit and was married to Doris Lax of Hallgarth Street in 1931. He died in April 1995.

Wounded soldiers at Brancepeth Castle, 7th Durham Voluntary Aid Detachment Hospital (VAD) 16 September 1915, prior to an outing to Richmond, North Yorkshire, arranged by Mr Luke Conlon. During World War One over 4,000 wounded soldiers were treated at the castle. (Taken by Austin Wood, Bishop Auckland.)

A Remembrance Day Service, Durham Cathedral, Sunday afternoon, 4 August 1918. This special service of prayer and thanksgiving was to comemorate the fourth anniversary of World War One. The civic procession was arranged by the Mayor Ald. Pattison and was headed by cadets and members of the Church Lads Brigade. A collection was made for the Durham Light Infantry Prisoner of War fund. (Taken by George Fillingham.)

One of the earliest aerial photographs of the city, photographed by the newly formed Royal Air Force (previously the RFC), taken at 12 noon on 24 October 1918. They were flying from their Training Depot Station, RAF Catterick (49 TDS). The smoking house fires of the city centre are very evident in this view.

A pewter 'Peace' medal given to all school children from the city who took part in celebrations at the end of the World War One. Despite the many that were given out, this is the only one the author has come across.

Brothers John William, left, and Walter Edwin Robinson, Durham Market Place, 1920s. They were both from No. 2 Mayorswell Street, Gilesgate, and had seen action in World War One. Walter served with the 9th West Riding Regiment and John was with the 7th Lincolnshire Regiment, Both were injured, with Walter receiving a shell wound to the face in 1916 and John suffering a heart condition. Notice the good shine on their boots, the mark of an old soldier.

Erecting Bede College's World War One memorial, 25 May 1922. Commemorating 86 men, it was unveiled on Bede Day, 27 May 1922, by Lt Col J.R. Ritson, TD. The cross was dedicated by Dr Herbert Hensley Henson, Bishop of Durham. (Taken by the City Studio, 69 Saddler Street.)

Gravenstafel Ridge, Flanders, 1920s, showing the spot where Bede Company were nearly wiped out on 25 April 1915. A third of the contingent were casualties, the rest were killed. Their names are recorded on the college war memorial.

The World War One memorial, Sherburn Hill, photographed on 22 October 1921, the day it was unveiled. It was dedicated by the Revd H.P. Boase, Wesleyan Minister, and unveiled by Major Arthur Dorman, managing director of the Colliery Co. The granite obelisk, made by Emley and Son, Newcastle, stands 12ft high and cost £300, paid for by public subscription. The names of those killed in World War Two were later added to the base.

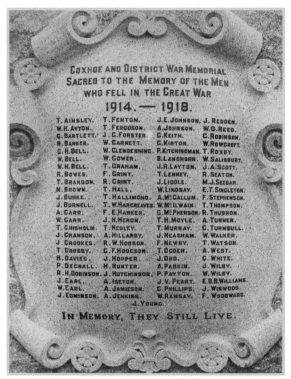

Coxhoe and District's granite World War One memorial, 1922. It was made by A.H. Borrowdale, Worksop, Nottingham, and unveiled in June 1922 by Sgt William Wilson, DCM and Bar. It was originally situated on the outer wall of the institute in Church Street. The names of those killed in World War Two were later added to the bottom on a small plaque. (Taken by Chisholm, Coxhoe.)

A period postcard of a certificate awarded to Mrs Bessie Cady by the Durham Voluntary Aid Organisation for valuable services rendered during World War One.

Witton Gilbert's World War One memorial in the early 1920s. The cross was designed by J.G. Burrell of Durham and cost £400. It was unveiled on 1 September 1922 by Lieut Col J.R. Ritson, TD, and dedicated by the Revd W.A. Elder, curate of Witton Gilbert. It was originally situated in Witton Dene but, unfortunately, due to vandalism, had to be moved to its present location near the junction with Briar Lea. It was rededicated on 5 November 1978. (Taken by The City Studio, Saddler Street.)

One of the two sections of the Ushaw Moor World War One memorial, then situated on the wall of the Memorial Hall, c.1920. It was unveiled on 3 October 1925 by Lieut Col J.R. Ritson, TD, and cost about £800. It is now located on the south wall of St Luke's Church, with the names of those killed in World War Two added. (Taken by A. Trelford, Ushaw Moor.)

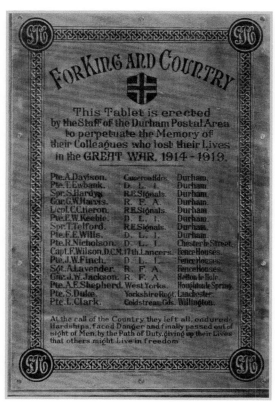

A period postcard of the Durham postal area's World War One memorial. It is a brass plaque mounted on oak, designed by W.T. Toulson, an engraver from Durham. It was unveiled on 2 August 1920 by the Mayor, W.H. Wood, and dedicated by Canon Dawson Dawson-Walker (see page 62). It was originally in the General Post Office, Saddler Street, then in 1929 it was moved to the new premises in Claypath. Finally, around 1995, it was placed in the waiting area of the postal sorting office, Belmont Industrial Estate.

Pilot Thomas Keith Kay Paul, Royal New Zealand Air Force, July 1943. He was a New Zealander whose mother (Mrs Isabella Paul, née Savage, a relative of the author) was born at Carrville. Paul enlisted in July 1940 as a trainee pilot in the NZAF. He came to England in September 1941, flying with 207 Sqn Bomber Command, taking part in many raids over Germany. He was killed while flying with the RAF on 4 January 1944, aged 26, when his Wellington bomber crashed in Brockhurst Wood on Farnham Common, Surrey, after hitting the cable of a barrage balloon on returning from a night-time training exercise. He was brought to Durham to be buried with his grandparents in St Oswald's cemetery. His fiancée, Miss Violet Dunn, living in New Zealand in 2007 gave Wellington College, NZ, a gift of $1.5 million in his memory.

Durham University Air Squadron Cadets (with Canadians) on Palace Green during World War Two. Students who joined could learn to fly and do other training while still studying for their degrees. During wartime most were then called up to become RAF aircrew.

A group from Croxdale Local Defence Volunteers (LDV, later renamed the Home Guard) 1942. The photograph was taken after a night-time exercise along the hedgerows of Croxdale and the surrounding area.

Durham University Air Squadron Cadets, Palace Green, 1939–45, taken during a rifle exercise. Photographs from this period are scarce due to the shortage of film during the war.

A group of soldiers from the 8th Battalion, Durham Light Infantry in Honiton, Devon, 1941. The weapon that the man in the front row is holding is a 'Tommy' submachine-gun, invented in the USA in 1919 by John T. Thompson.

Two soldiers of the Royal Marines pose with the Wakenshaw anti-tank gun, Tobruk, 1944. The photograph is signed on the reverse and was taken by 'RM'. Pte Adam Wakenshaw, 9th Battalion, Durham Light Infantry was killed on 27 June 1942 south of Mersa Matruh, while using this gun. He was posthumously awarded the Victoria Cross for his bravery. After the war a street on the newly built council estate, Sunderland Road (Gilesgate), was named in his honour. The gun is now on display in the DLI Museum.

One of the 'Aycliffe Angels' (munitions workers), Isabella Bailey (née Ellis), *c*.1942, pictured climbing the outside wooden staircase in the courtyard of No. 149 Gilesgate, a tenement block situated to the left of St Giles's Church drive. Only six days before VE Day, 2 May 1945, she was killed in an explosion at the Royal Ordnance Factory at Aycliffe, along with seven others. This is the only photograph her son Bill (see page 171) has of his mother.

Driver Charles Henry Piper, T/13023670, Royal Army Service Corps, c.1940. He was the only son of Alf Piper, a grocer from High Pittington and husband of Vera. Piper was killed on 16 March 1945, aged 30. His remains were later reburied at Coriano Ridge War Cemetery, Italy, along with other fallen comrades.

Mr R. Roxborough in the yard of No. 32 Lawson Terrace, c.1939. Prior to the outbreak of World War Two Roxborough was employed at Shire Hall, Old Elvet. The masking tape on the window was to prevent shards of glass flying if they were shattered during bombing raids.

Merchant Seaman, Fourth Engineer Kenneth Greenwell, from Sacriston, c.1940. He was a frequent letter-writer to the Children's Corner of *The Durham County Advertiser* in the 1930s, telling of his worldly travels, signing himself as 'Captain Kay'. He died on 23 November 1942 aged 30 when his ship, the SS *Goolistan*, was torpedoed by *U-625* 300 miles off North Cape, with the loss of all hands. The ship was returning from Archangel as part of a Russian Convoy. His poem *Arctic Convoy, A Saga of the Sea*, was published in book form by *The Durham County Advertiser* in October 1943.

A presentation of proficiency certificates and badges to members of the Johnston Flight No. 234 Squadron (Durham) Air Training Corps (ATC) 5 October 1942, photographed in the yard of Durham Johnston School, South Street. The headmaster of the school, Dr Christopher Storey, the Mayor, H.L. Gradon (chairman of the ATC committee for the Durham area), and Flight-Lieut, H. Cecil Ferens, can all be seen. (Taken by George Fillingham.)

Soldiers of the 8th Battalion, Durham Light Infantry (Territorials), from Gilesgate Drill Hall, October 1958. Major James Mulhall had been visiting outlying villages with some of his men, looking for new recruits to swell the ranks, with the tempting offer of a free pint of beer and 'a bit crack' back at the drill hall. Second from the right, seated, is World War Two veteran, Nicholas (Nicky) Owens, originally from Sacriston. He moved to Gilesgate when he married Nora Coyle.

Mr William Hartley, senior verger at Durham Cathedral, in 1867. He possessed extensive knowledge on the history of the cathedral and was highly respected by Dean Waddington, whom he served for many years. When the Dean died on 20 July 1869, he left Hartley £2,000, a small fortune in those days. Hartley died on 22 April 1876.

Mr John Moor, verger at Durham Cathedral, 1867. Prior to becoming a verger in the cathedral he was general factotum (servant) to Archdeacon Thorp, warden of the university. He was also sworn in as watchman and special constable for the university on 19 January 1836. He served as verger for 36 years and did not retire until 1874. Moor died on 9 January 1875.

The restoration of the east end of the Chapter House, Durham Cathedral, c.1895. It had been destroyed in 1776 by order of the Chapter, acting upon the advice of Mr James Wyatt, cathedral architect, despite it once being described as 'the finest Norman chapter house in England'. The restoration work was carried out under the direction of the Dean and the Chapter's architect, Mr C. Hodgson Fowler. It was finished and dedicated in June 1895 as a memorial to the late Bishop Lightfoot.

Police Constable 321 John Kirkup on the left, and PC 376 Thomas Snaith on the right, *c.*1885. PC Kirkup had joined the force in 1869 and was stationed at Sherburn Village between 1877–88. On the 15 March 1882 PC Kirkup was fined 20 shillings and cautioned for drinking and spending his time in a public house when on duty. PC Snaith had joined in June 1883 and was stationed at Lanchester, transferring to Durham HQ in 1885. Prior to January 1899, officers were required at all times, whether on or off duty, to appear in their regulation uniform unless otherwise directed. (Taken by W. Wilkinson, then operating at No. 7 Atherton Street.)

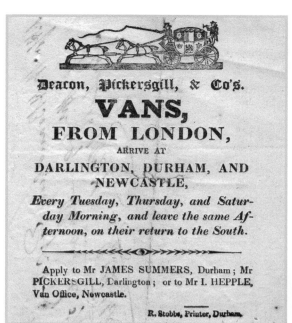

A rare coach service hand-bill from Deacon Pickersgill & Co., *c.*1829. It was printed by R. Stobbs, Durham. The local agent was Mr James Summers, The Warehouse, Durham Market Place. The daily pick-up and drop-off points for London were at Darlington, Durham and Newcastle.

A brass Durham Corporation street trader's licence, *c.*1906. It is thought to be a prototype, as no others are known. This example is in unused condition. It would have been worn attached to a leather strap fastened to the forearm.

An unknown carter with his son, *c.*1883. The photograph was taken by W. Wilkinson, who was born in Bishop Auckland in 1853 and grew up in Willington. He spent 10 years working at the mine before moving to Broompark and starting his professional career. Firstly operating at No. 7 Atherton Street, Wilkinson later moved to 83 North Road in the late 1880s, then to No. 21 Silver Street and finally Nos. 50 and 57 Saddler Street. His work was highly regarded at the time. He died on 3 December 1919.

A postcard advertising Thomas Shadforth, an auctioneer, valuer, house furnisher and general hardware man of Nos. 12 and 75 North Road, *c*.1906. The premises on the left, were demolished and rebuilt in the same style several years ago. The ground floor is now Burger King. The property on the right was near to where the present Yates's Wine Lodge stands.

Mr G.J. Fillingham, provision and hardware dealer, of No. 50 North Road, in the late 1920s. Adverts in the window are for Berna Swiss Milk, Rowntree's Cocoa, Sunlight Soap and Brito Margarine. (Taken by Sidney E. Taylor, No. 5 Silver Street.)

The shop front of George Greenwell's premises, 1880s. Greenwell was a grocer, tea dealer and wine and spirit merchant, from Albert House, No. 33 Silver Street. The window display tells the story of the history of tea. The label in the top-left corner shows the address of his earlier shop at No. 5. He opened his first shop in 1849 (see 1850 *Durham Directory*, printed in 1849), he moved to No. 33 Silver Street in 1851. In 1887 as a lasting memorial to Queen Victoria's golden jubilee, he had two blocks of marble fitted to the frontage of the shop with the dates 1837–1887. The shop closed in 1983 after 133 years in the Greenwell hands. The premises are now occupied by the main post office.

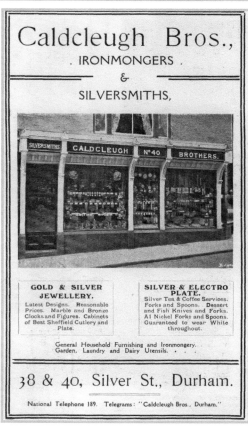

Caldcleugh Brothers', ironmongers and silversmiths, at Nos. 38 and 40 Silver Street, c.1909. The property was originally the 17th-century town house of Sir John Duck (Durham's Dick Whittington). It was, regrettably, demolished in the 1960s and replaced by a nondescript building.

A Christmas scene showing the shop frontage at Brown's (Newcastle Ltd) fishmonger, game and poultry dealers, at No. 24 Silver Street, *c.*1907. (Taken by W. Wilkinson.)

The Durham Café, No. 5 Saddler Street, in the 1900s. The signs in the window read 'Ladies' Tea Room Upstairs' and 'High Class Refreshments'. The business was part of a branch run by The North of England Café Company Ltd.

Lockey's Stores & Cafe. . .

Five Minutes' Walk from Cathedral and Castle.

76, Saddler St., Durham City.

LOCKEY'S CAFE IS CENTRAL AND COMFORTABLE AND HAS EVERY ACCOMMODATION.

LOCKEY'S FAMOUS TEAS——
Awarded the Gold Medal and Diploma for Tea Blending, London, 1907.
Awarded the Silver Medal and Diploma for Tea Blending, London, 1908.
Nat. Tel. 35. **Lockey's Stores & Café, Durham.**

An advert for Lockey's supply stores and café at No. 76 Saddler Street, *c.*1909. Lockey's were noted for their famous teas. The premises are now the Northern Rock Building Society. The Lockey family lived at Rosslea House, Gilesgate, near Baths Bridge, now in the grounds of Bede College.

The shop front of James Fowler, high class grocer (established 1841), at No. 99 Claypath in the 1920s. Some may recall the smell of freshly ground coffee beans as you passed the premises and the ramped entrance down into the shop. The premises were situated almost opposite the present Millennium Place and were taken down prior to the new Claypath underpass being constructed in the early 1960s.

Mr T. Wilson, a grocer of No. 31 New Elvet, *c*.1908. The shop stood near to where the present retail premises are situated, opposite Dunelm House. His son, Henry, later ran the business.

Opposite: Mr John Howarth Jnr, 'public window cleaner', with his collection of ladders outside the premises of 'John Howarth, dealer in furniture', No. 11 Elvet Bridge, in 1907. Note the lady leaning out of the top window. In the distance, above No 73 Saddler Street, is a sign for the Croft Hotel. The shop on the right was the Premier Trading Stamp Co., and the lettering on the window reads 'No Goods Sold Here, All Goods Given Away'.

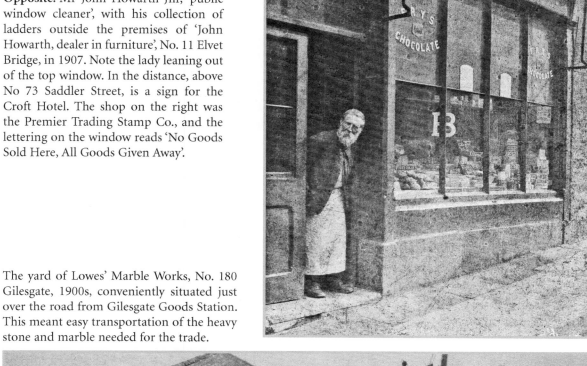

The yard of Lowes' Marble Works, No. 180 Gilesgate, 1900s, conveniently situated just over the road from Gilesgate Goods Station. This meant easy transportation of the heavy stone and marble needed for the trade.

The rear of the old stables and outbuildings belonging to W.H. Wood, later Wood and Watson Ltd, No. 132 Gilesgate, 1890s. These were destroyed in a fire on 30 June 1901, when eight out of their 20 horses were killed.

An early staff photograph from W.H. Wood, mineral water manufacturer on Gilesgate, 1890s. They joined Mr J. Watson, Wood's brother-in-law, around 1903 and became Wood and Watson Ltd. Standing on the extreme left is W.H. Wood. Other people in the group include Henry Lightfoot, Bob Glover, Ethel McGregor, Mr Burt, Joe Wood and Lizzie Gilson, née Foster.

An early motorised wagon, belonging to Wood and Watson Ltd of No. 132 Gilesgate, 1920s. The photograph was taken outside Slake Terrace public house, West Cornforth.

The state of the art bottling plant in Wood and Watson's factory, 1930s. At the time of the photograph, 15 girls and two men were employed in the factory. They had four lorries, run by five men, each with their own wagon boy, delivering all over the county, especially the coastal areas. (Taken by John Edis.)

Two workers from Wood and Watson's in the early 1950s. On the left is Bobby Thompson, driver, and wagon lad, Tommy Rowntree. The photograph was taken at Coundon, Bishop Auckland, while on their delivery round. Many will remember Tommy as the university postman, a job he held for almost 17 years until his retirement.

The office staff of Wood and Watson's 'pop' factory, 1960. From left to right: Audrey Dent, Vera Robinson, Mrs Anderson, Teresa Crawford and Miss Wallace, the secretary. The front office site is now occupied by a new house facing the 'Duck Pond' at Gilesgate Green.

Staff from Wood and Watson's 'pop' factory, 1950s, photographed in the old lane leading to St Giles's churchyard behind the former factory. On the right is the author's relative, Peter Kelly.

A Leyland wagon from Wood and Watson's delivering to the Neville Dene Hotel, 1950s. Above the cab of the van is an advert for their new drink, 'Watcheer'. The hotel was later renamed The Pot and Glass, after the old pub on Toll House Road. It has recently changed its name again, to The Lodge. (Taken by Daisy Edis.)

Durham miners' officials, photographed in the council chamber of the Durham Miners' Hall, Red Hill, *c.*1916. The hall was capable of seating almost 400 people. (Taken by W. Wilkinson.)

One of *The Durham County Advertiser* photographers, Frank Bilton, 1960s, taken in the yard behind the old newspaper office in Saddler Street. He started with the paper after leaving Whinney Hill School and had clocked up over 45 years for the paper. Now retired, Frank is a familiar sight at civic events as one of the Mayor's bodyguards.

The Patterson triplets, Walter, Arthur and Frederick, from Gilesgate Moor, who all worked at MacKay's Carpet factory, March 1936. Two of the brothers played football for the factory team.

Mr Herby Newton with his brother's horse outside the Marine Stores (dealer in rags, bones, scrap iron and jars), 1930s. This was his brother's second yard, and it was near Gilesgate Goods Station. The first yard was on the site of the old Kepier Colliery, next to the 'Duff Heap' (a waste site containing small coals), Sunderland Road. Herby's brother, Charlie, left there after the old shaft had opened up and took away his shed, along with several thousand jam jars.

One of Charlie Newton's fruit and vegetable carts, seen in the 'stable yard', Sherburn Road Ends, late 1930s. The old building behind was later converted into a house. A Dalmatian dog can be seen behind the cart.

A fruit and vegetable cart belonging to Charlie Newton, taken at Sherburn Road Ends opposite the 'stable yard', 1930s. The lettering on the cart reads 'English and Foreign Fruiterer'. A flower bed and motorist discount shop now occupy the site of the old Co-operative store.

A fruit and vegetable cart at the side of the 'store corner' on Sherburn Road Ends, late 1930s. Charlie Newton hired out horses and carts to local hawkers. His son, Charlie Jnr, was a successful scrap metal merchant, and he lived in a luxurious 1960s house on Broomside Lane, Belmont (now demolished), which featured in the film *Get Carter*, starring Michael Caine.

A United double-decker open-top bus with the destination plate for Durham, *c*.1913. Half of the company's fleet was requisitioned during World War One and sent to France to carry troops.

A North Eastern Railway (NER) bus outside the old entrance of Durham Railway Station, *c*.1911. On the reverse of the postcard is written 'Leo and his conductor'. Note the solid tyres.

Mr George Larke with his Lyons' Tea delivery van, November 1935. He was then living at No. 63 Gilesgate and using the former shop for the storage of tea. His vehicle was garaged near Gilesgate Goods Station.

James Laidler and Son, automobile engineers, No. 83 New Elvet, *c.*1909. The firm were more famous as engineers, brass founders, plumbers and for their miners' safety lamps, which now command a high price at auction.

The horse-drawn showman's caravan, adapted for use by the Church Army Diocesan Mission, 1930s. It was a familiar sight around the villages. They are listed in the Durham Diocesan Calendar 1935 as having two vans working in the Durham area.

The new 'dustbin wagon' (an Eagle hydraulic-end lifting refuse collector) belonging to Durham Rural District Council, 1937. The starting handle at the front was used for cranking up the engine manually.

David Larke next to his father's delivery van outside No. 64 Whinney Hill, August 1948. The van has an unusual roll-top sliding door fitted on the side, advertising 'Bev', one of their products.

David Larke standing next to his father's Lyons Tea van outside No. 133 Gilesgate, *c*.1947. From modest beginnings as supplier of catering to the Newcastle Exhibition in 1887, this new firm rapidly expanded. When their first tea shops were opened they provided a ready outlet for their own blend. This business soon became popular, and the Joe Lyons Corner Houses and tea shops, with their 'Nippy' waitresses, became a household name.

The No. 53 United bus from Merry Oaks travelling over Framwellgate Bridge towards the Market Place, 1950s. On the extreme left is the old Criterion public house, and in the background is Alexander the Jeweller.

A diesel goods-train passing Belmont Junction, Carrville, going onto the line branching off to Gilesgate Goods Station, *c*.1966. In the background, crossing the photograph, is the railway embankment leading to Brasside (Belmont) Viaduct.

A group of workers from Mattesons sausage factory (now Kerry Foods), Gilesgate Moor, 1979. In the centre is Nicky Owens (see page 80) and front far-right is Jean Blackburn. Other names in the group include John Chester, Frances Logan, Martha Williams, Irene, Jean Robinson, Dolly Short, David Williams, Pat Logan and Belle Hutton. (Taken by Fillinghams.)

The bronze replica 'sanctuary knocker' being placed on the north door of the cathedral, February 1980. The original (now displayed in the Cathedral Treasury), dating from *c.*1140, had been taken down in December 1977, it was and sent to the British Museum, London, for restoration. While there, this copy was made and both appeared on the *Blue Peter* children's TV show. In the Middle Ages, the Cathedral provided a haven for fugitives. Anyone who had committed a serious offence could claim sanctuary by knocking on the door. They would then be given 37 days to organise their affairs. After this they had to decide either to stand trial or leave the country by the nearest port. It was reported in *The Durham County Advertiser*, September 1942, that the knocker had been vandalised, the culprits having painted it red, white and blue.

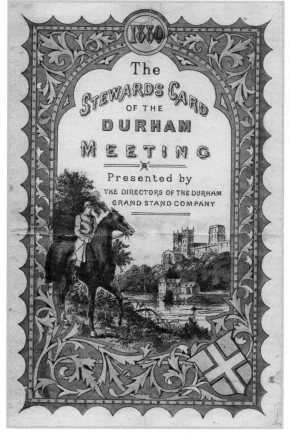

The Stewards' Card for Durham Race Meeting, Easter Tuesday, 30 March, 1880. This attractive card was printed in colour by W. Ainsley & Bro., Waddington Street, Durham City. One of the largest meetings ever recorded was on 14 April 1873. *The Durham County Advertiser* reported crowds of around 80,000 attending the two-day event. All lodging houses were full and many chose to sleep in passages and shop doorways. Some local people made a few shillings by letting folk sleep in armchairs in their homes.

The Racecourse, viewed from the grounds of St Hild's College in the 1880s. Horse-racing was held here from about 1733. Before that time, as far back as the 1600s, race meetings were at Framwellgate Moor, Brasside Moor and Durham Moor. The huge crowds attracted travelling showmen and shooting-gallery stalls. In the 1881 census many of the showmen are listed as occupants of The Racecourse, where they had set up their caravans and tents.

THE DURHAM REGATTA.

An early 19th-century engraving from *The Illustrated London News* showing Prebends Bridge. The occasion was the Durham Regatta, one of the oldest in the country, officially founded 1834. River festivals began in 1815 to celebrate the victory of Waterloo, and it is recorded that this event continued on Waterloo Day each year and formed the foundation for the present regatta.

A Victorian silver medal (struck in 1839) presented to individual winning crews at the Durham Regatta in 1875. It was awarded to the four crew of Durham School. The names on the reverse are Delavel Knight Gregson, Frederick Alexander Bowlby, John Harbottle Nicholson, Lewis Ward and Algernon Grey (cox). This example has the date 1875, which is five years after it was thought to have ceased to be given.

An 18ct gold Wharton Challenge Cup medal, presented at the Durham Regatta in 1895. The cup was given by the Rt Hon John Lloyd Wharton in 1877. It was awarded to the winner of the four-oared race, restricted to one crew from each of the following: Durham Amateur Rowing Club, Durham University, Durham School and Bede College. It was rowed on the long course. This example still has the original Victorian case from Caldcleugh Jewellers, No. 38 Silver Street.

The old iron Baths Bridge on Regatta Day, 24 June 1905, showing the officials' box mounted on the bridge. At the Corporation Meeting, January 1903, Mr H.E. Ferens raised the matter of the gas lights on and near the bridge being constantly 'put out' by young lads. Alderman Battensby said the lads wanted a good stick taking to their backs.

Durham Regatta from Pelaw Woods, 24 June 1905. Musical arrangements this year for the promenade on The Racecourse were provided by the band of the Royal Irish Fusiliers from Dublin. Because of the long exposure time of the camera, the rowers appear as two blurs on the water.

St Cuthbert's Boat Club's senate crew, epiphany term, 1911. Standing, left to right: W.H. Webb (bow) and E.B. Alban (stroke). Seated, left to right: H.P. Young (3), D.S. Davies (cox) and W.J.R. Sherlock (2). (Taken by John Edis.)

Bede College maiden four-oared crew, winners of the Durham Amateur Rowing Club At Home, 4 June 1910.
Standing, left to right: Johnston (bow), Musgrave (capt), Pinkney (3). Seated, left to right: Moore (2), Marriott
(stroke) and Smith (cox).

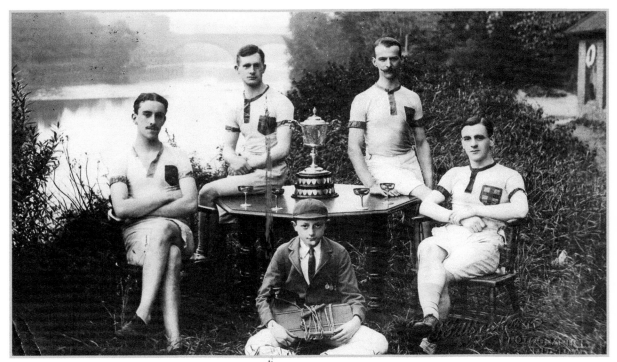

Durham Amateur Rowing Club (established 1860), winners of the Tyne General Ferry Challenge Cup, Tyne Regatta, held at Scotswood, 20 July 1912. They are pictured next to University College boathouse, near the Fulling Mill, now the Archaeological Museum. The crew are: C.C. Heron (bow), N. Darling, R. Levitt, R. Mitcham (stroke) and Wood (cox). (Taken by George Fillingham.)

Winners of The Lowe Memorial Challenge Bowl, Durham Regatta, 14 June 1932. Left to right: E.S. Nelson (cox), J.R. Thurlow (stroke), C.A. Riley, M. Phelan and T.W. Allen (bow). Photographed at University College boathouse, near the Fulling Mill.

Durham University Boat Club, 1951. Back row, left to right: G. Semb (7), D.L. Craven (stroke) and J. Stockill (6). Front row: B. Brown (coach), D.A. Helliwell (5), M.J. Fry (3), J.E. Chaston (cox), P.C. Murray (bow), B. Lodge (2) and A. Serk-Hansen (4).

Friends and family of Tommy Wilson, landlord of the Dun Cow public house, Old Elvet, photographed at the Durham Regatta, c.1966. Left to right: Steve O'Donnell, Micky Brown, Billy Cawood, Ken, Neville Boyd, Gordon Anderson, Melvin Carr, Tommy Wilson, Billy Mitchell, Alan Bellerby, Audrey Wilson, Jackie Parkin, Bob Robson and Janice Wilson at the front.

The President's Prize, a silver medal awarded to J. Morson Jnr for excellence at Durham City Camera Club in 1903. The medal was made by T. Brewster, Durham. The club was founded in 1892, and continued until around the start of World War One.

The 'Royal Waxworks' of John Manders at the Easter Fair, The Sands, April 1904. He was also one of the early cinema pioneers, showing 'Edison's Electric Animated Pictures' to the masses. He added moving pictures to his waxworks exhibition in 1899. The first showing was at the Newcastle Christmas Fair.

The brightly painted shuggy (or swing) boats at the Easter Fair, The Sands, April 1904. By pulling on their ropes alternately, the rider could swing the boat up to a great height. Unfortunately this is no longer a feature, thanks to health and safety regulations.

Easter Fair, The Sands, April 1904. On the skyline to the left is Kepier House (situated behind The Chains, Gilesgate), which was originally the Durham County Penitentiary (St Mary's Home).

A procession of Freemasons leaving the main entrance of Durham Castle, 20 October 1880. The occasion was the appointment of the Most Honourable the Marquess of Londonderry to the position of Provincial Grand Master of the Province.

The horse fair, Old Elvet, 1890s. The event was normally held in March each year. Behind is the Waterloo Hotel, managed by T. Weavers, and on the right is the Royal County Hotel. (Taken by W. Wilkinson.)

The funeral cortège for the Revd Canon George Body DD (see page 55), Canon Missioner of Durham, leaving the north door of the cathedral, 8 June 1911. Born on 7 January 1840 at Cheriton Fitzpaine, Devon, where his father was a surgeon, he was educated at Blundells School, Tiverton, and St John's College, Cambridge. He took holy orders in 1863 and a year later was priest at Lichfield. (Taken by W. Wilkinson.)

The grave of the Revd Canon Body in Durham Cathedral Churchyard, 8 June 1911. The ornate stone cross unfortunately no longer stands; it is now laid flat on the grave. (Taken by W. Wilkinson.)

A sketch of coal miners at the corner of King Street (now North Road), near Millburngate, March 1892. The group is discussing the state of affairs during the miners' strike against the reduction of wages. Over 92,000 coal miners from the county came out in support.

Saddler Street, decorated for the coronation of George V, 22 June 1911. On the right is a cart belonging to Walter Wilson's store. The business premises on the left are Hiller's music shop, Coyne's children's outfitter, the House of Andrews book shop and Lockey's supply store and café. On the opposite side of the road is the large sign of The North of England Café (see page 86).

The coronation parade coming into the Market Place from the direction of Silver Street, 22 June 1911. The smartly dressed children are probably from St Margaret's School in Margery Lane. A cathedral service took place for children at 9.30am, and in the afternoon sports were held at Hollow Drift, near The Racecourse. Note the third pant base on the right, erected in 1902.

A band from the 8th Battalion, Durham Light Infantry, playing in the Market Place during the coronation festivities, 22 June 1911. In the background, centre right, is the Market Hotel and the main entrance to the indoor market.

A coronation party held in Kepier Gardens, attached to the farm, 22 June 1911. The postcard had been sent to Edie from Polly. In the background on the right are the ruins of the old manor house of the Heaths. The ground floor, with its Elizabethan arcade, still survives. (Taken by George Fillingham.)

A hallmarked silver medal given to dignitaries by Lord and Lady Londonderry during their time as Mayor and Mayoress of Durham. At a summer fête in the grounds of Seaham Hall, 31 August 1911, all 3,000 schoolchildren from the city were give a pewter version of the same medal. On arrival at the grounds they were all given a pie and a bottle of lemonade. Afternoon tea consisted of a hot cup of tea and a bag of cakes.

A presentation to Edward, Prince of Wales, at Durham Railway Station, 26 November 1897. Henry Collins (see page 57) is seen presenting a pick-axe to the Prince. Mr Collins had held this item in his possession for almost 40 years. It had been used by the Prince as a young man while on a visit to Houghton Pit, part of the Lambton estates, on 19 May 1857.

The visit of Daudi Chwa II, Kabaka of Buganda (the largest of the Western Region of Uganda), to Durham, July 1913 (he spent several days in Durham). He ascended to the throne in August 1897, and at the time of his coronation he was one years old. He is pictured near 'Windy Gap' in the south-west corner of Palace Green. The king, aged about 16, was accompanied by two of his leading chiefs, Tefiro Musalosale and Semeno Kasuja, as guests of Bishop Tucker (see page 59) He died on 22 November 1939. (Taken by George Fillingham.)

Queen Mary's visit to Shincliffe Aged Miners' Homes, 26 November 1913. The lady in the doorway is Mrs Turnbull, an aged widow from No. 6 Bells Street. The gentleman leading the group is Mr John Wilson, Labour MP for Mid-Durham. The settlement then known as Shincliffe Colliery, and later as Shincliffe Bank Top, has been called High Shincliffe since 1 April 1969. (Taken by George Fillingham.)

A military guard of honour lining Saddler Street on 11 November 1920. The occasion was the consecration, presentation and laying up of the colours belonging to 13 battalions of the Durham Light Infantry in Durham Cathedral. The cars were carrying the Earl of Durham, Major Gen. Sir Percy Wilkinson (C.O. Northumbrian Division), Lt Gen. Sir Francis Robb, Brig. Gen. H.R. Cumming, Brig. Gen. H. Conyers Surtees and Lt Col Hugh Bowes. The street was lined with 350 men of the D.L.I.

A property in New Elvet decorated for the Silver Jubilee of King George and Queen Mary, 1935. On the extreme left is the County Council Health Office, No. 81 New Elvet, and next to it is No. 82 the office of the North of England Joint Insurance Prescription Committee. The ground floor of the latter is now a coffee bar. Many will remember the ground floor as Embletons garage and petrol station. The doors on the right belonged to the Waterloo Hotel garage. The hotel (see page 162) stood to the left of the Royal County Hotel in Old Elvet.

The royal visit of King George VI and Queen Elizabeth to Sherburn Road Estates, 23 February 1939. Receiving the royal party was the Mayor, Wilf Edge, and, with his back to the camera in the centre front, Lord Londonderry. The photograph was taken on the bottom estate, near the area known as the 'Bull Ring'.

Mr Matthew Keating (1869–1937) MP speaking at the annual Irish Gala, Wharton Park, Durham, 5 August 1912. The event was organised by the Durham branches of the United Irish League of Great Britain and had been established a number of years. *The Durham County Advertiser* reported the event and praised the fact that despite hundreds of the 'Irish race' attending there were no arrests. The Irish politician was elected for South Kilkenny at the by-election of 1909. The speaker and some of his audience are photographed dangerously perched on the edge of the open-air amphitheatre.

The Mayor and Mayoress of Durham, Lord and Lady Londonderry, visiting Harrison's organ factory, Hawthorn Terrace, Durham City, 28 August 1911. After looking around they were entertained to lunch in the castle by the Master of University College, Dr Henry Gee. This was one of many engagements that day, which ended with a garden party at The Laurels, Sherburn Road Ends, the home of the Deputy Mayor W.H. Wood. (Taken by Speedy Photo. Co., Durham.)

The visit of Charlie Chaplin to Durham. He was photographed in the castle courtyard with Vice-Master of University College, Dr W.A. Prowse, prior to receiving his honorary DLitt degree from the university, 6 July 1962.

The Durham City Rovers cycling club (see page 124), first-prize winners at the lifeboat procession for the Royal National Lifeboat Institution, photographed on Palace Green, 31 May 1905. The parade assembled at the barracks field, Gilesgate, and travelled through the city towards The Racecourse. Note the fine selection of costumes and the two donkeys, complete with jockeys.

'Our motor wedding', the first prize in the lifeboat procession, 1905. The picture shows a motorcycle and wicker sidecar, an entry from Lyons Café, No. 39 Silver Street, Durham. The postcard states they are 'noted for their bride's cakes'.

Student rag parade, 'Durham Derby', at Palace Green, Monday 23 June 1913. The procession was headed by Herr Von Blowithobitz and his Palatinate Hungarian Band. The buildings in the background are Cosin's Hall on the left and the Alms' Houses on the right. (Taken by George Fillingham.)

Herr Von Blowithobitz, seen on the left, with his rather large moustache, holding his bandsman's stick and wearing a sash, 23 June 1913. He is accompanied by some of his Palatinate Hungarian Band. The photograph was taken on Palace Green by George Fillingham prior to the start of the parade.

The student rag parade, 23 June 1913. The procession, led by Von Blowithobitz is seen coming over Framwellgate Bridge in the direction of North Road. The parade would go as far as the County Hospital then turn back towards Palace Green. (Taken by George Fillingham.)

Entrants for the student rag parade in the castle courtyard, c.1913. Pram races were one of the parade's regular features. In May of 1913 special watchmen were appointed at the castle by the university, owing to the recent suffragette scare. (Taken by George Fillingham.)

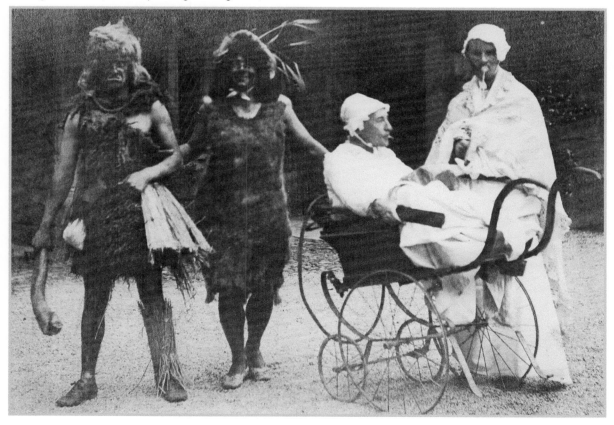

Students dressed as druids for the rag parade at Palace Green, 24 June 1922. The theme this year was the marriage of Caesar and Boadicea. Palace Green had been transformed by the students to represent Stonehenge. A street collection raised £78 for the Durham County Hospital. Top left is Owengate (Queen Street), the main entrance to Palace Green. (Taken by George Fillingham.)

A 'battered rugby team', an entry for the student rag, June 1928. The students raised £120 for the County Hospital and £80 for the Castle Restoration Fund. During the day an aeroplane did a handbill drop over the city, appealing for help. A pram race also took place in Old Elvet.

Durham University Officer Training Corps, 4 November 1913. The occasion was the conferring of honorary degrees. The procession was seen after the ceremony in the castle courtyard. Left to right: Sir George Hare Philipson, Pro-Vice Chancellor, unknown, Arthur James Balfour (Prime Minister, 1902–05) DCL and unknown.

Ladies' Day at Durham City Bowling Club, the Racecourse, July 1915. The man on the left with a tea cup is Mr Fred Howarth (see page 145), headmaster of Bluecoat School. (Taken by George Fillingham.)

'Ladies Day', an outing from Durham City Rovers Cycling Club, photographed at Blackhall Rocks, 1 June 1913. The group, which was founded in 1897, held its meetings in the Criterion Hotel, near Framwellgate Bridge.

The coach carrying Mr Justice Grantham leaving the cathedral for the Assize Court, *c.*1904. His Honour's views on prisons were published in *The British Medical Journal* from 31 March 1888: 'Our gaols are in too sanitary a condition; our prisoners are too comfortable'. A residence in prison was, according to Mr Justice Grantham, 'rather a pleasure than a punishment'.

Dignitaries of the County of Durham Assizes in the castle courtyard, 3 July 1917. Left to right: Archdeacon of Auckland, Percy Augustus Derry, Mr Justice McLandie, Lord Coleridge and unknown. The cost for the judges' lodgings for this year was £140. (Taken by John Edis.)

The chauffeur-driven car of the Assize Judge, with an unmounted police escort, pictured in the courtyard of Durham Castle, late 1920s. The Summer Assize Court was held each June for four weeks in the Crown Courts, Old Elvet. (Taken by 'Ernest' (Rawes), No. 21 Silver Street.)

The Venerable Archdeacon of Auckland, Percy Augustus Derry, pictured on the left pushing off the ball at the Federated Deaf Club's sports day, Bank Holiday Monday, 1927. On the right is the committee and team. Archdeacon Derry died on 13 October 1928.

Soldiers of the 8th Battalion, Durham Light Infantry, leading a parade through Gilesgate, *c*.1932. The large fronted building on the left is the old Brewer's Arms public house, now unfortunately student accomodation. On the right of it is Heron's wet fish shop and then Elgy's timber-yard.

A Labour May Day demonstration, led by a brass band, coming over Framwellgate Bridge, May 1907. On the left is a billboard advertising Herrings Hatter and Hosier, Established 1838. On 1 May 1920 all Durham miners observed the occasion as a general holiday.

A fine view of the huge crowds on The Racecourse at the Durham Miners' Gala, c.1911. In the top-left corner are the two rows of houses of Whinney Terrace. These were later demolished and the site is now occupied by the new prison gatehouse and car park.

Crowds coming down North Road, during Durham Miners' Gala, 18 July 1908. They are led by the Brandon Colliery banner, which bear the portraits of Alderman James Fowler, grocer No. 99 Claypath, five-times Mayor of Durham, and Mr Whitley, lodge secretary. This is the only known image of this particular banner, which was recorded in *The Durham County Advertiser* as being present at the 1893 gala. (Taken by W. Wilkinson.)

A procession of coal-miners and their families at the Durham Miners' Gala, 22 July 1911, taken from near the Shire Hall. They are travelling towards The Racecourse. In the foreground are two whippet dogs, a breed very popular with the miner.

Bowburn miners' banner and band on The Racecourse at the Durham Miners' Gala, 1920s. It bears the portrait of John Wilson MP. The bass drum has 'Bowburn Jaz Band 1919' painted on it. Jazz was the latest craze, following a sensational tour of Britain by the 'Original Dixieland Jazz Band' in 1919, which included a command performance for King George V at Buckingham Palace.

The lodge banner of South Pelaw and their union band on The Racecourse at the 'Big Meeting', 25 July 1925. The pit had opened in 1890 and closed on 2 January 1964. On the reverse is written, 'Bill Forster carried the banner, with five other men.' The college of St Hild is on the top left, and Pelaw Wood is on the right.

Kibblesworth miners and their families gather in front of the lodge banner on The Racecourse at the Durham Miner's Gala in the1920s. The banner is draped in black, signifying a death in the colliery since the last gala.

Madame Litricia, 'high class character reader, society palmist and clairvoyant', pictured at the Durham Miners' Gala on The Racecourse in the late 1930s.

A horse parade entrant from Fentiman's Botanical Brewers, Prospect Works, Hallgarth Street, standing near the tithe barn opposite Hallgarth Farm, *c.*1907. Although established by John Fentiman around 1903, Mr Broughton became owner in about 1908. Later the two families became linked through marriage.

A heavy rolley belonging to the North Eastern Railway Company, with its driver, Robert William Hall, of Gilesgate, c.1910. The occasion was the Durham City Horse Parade, held in the barracks field, Gilesgate. Behind is the factory of Wood and Watson Ltd, mineral water manufacturers. On the central left edge a horse is seen grazing; this field later became the 1927 churchyard for St Giles'.

An entrant from Claypath Co-operative Society at the Durham City Horse Parade, held in the barracks field, Gilesgate, in 1913. Spectators of all ages took advantage of the high barracks' wall to view the proceedings. The leading horse, known as 'a chain horse', was used to help heavy carts up banks, and they also acted as a brake, attached to the rear of carts, when going down steep inclines.

Entrants from the butchers' department of the Co-operative Society, with their horses and carts, at the Durham City Horse Parade, pictured in the barracks field, Gilesgate, 1914. On the extreme left is a cart from the Moor Edge Laundry. The horse on the right, with three prize tickets, was 20 years old (details from the reverse of the postcard).

Mr Robbie Hall, on the right, with two chestnuts belonging to Mrs Elizabeth English, Hall Farm, Front Street, Sherburn Village, taken at the Durham City Horse Parade, 1911. On the left, behind the group, is the old gatehouse of the barracks. Beyond that is the 'Duck Pond' area (Gilesgate Green).

A cart decorated with rolls of chicken wire, belonging to George Forster, ironmonger, No. 2 Market Place, *c.*1910. It was an entrant for the Durham City Horse Parade. The business was founded by Mr John Oliver and was taken over by George Forster in 1854. In 1892 it was acquired by W.B. Forster. Behind is the old militia barracks, now Vane Tempest Hall. (Taken by George Fillingham.)

A rolley (cart) belonging to Mrs Mildred Shepherd, Arbour House Farm, near Crossgate Moor, an entrant for the Durham City Horse Parade, 1927. The photograph was taken in the barracks field by George Fillingham.

The stand of George Forster at the Durham County Show in the late 1920s. The central display box holds a collection of various carborundum stones, used for sharpening implements. They were frequent prize winners at the County Shows for the best collection of dairy appliances.

An aerial photograph of a train crash on the main line at Browney Signal Box, between Ferryhill and Durham, 5 January 1946. A London to Newcastle express crashed into freight trucks, which had broken away from a goods train at 5.40am. Ten passengers were killed, and 18 had to be taken to hospital. This image was wired across the Atlantic to the New York Bureau and was found in the USA by the author.

St Godric's Church fire, 14 January 1985. A 13-year-old local youth had started the fire in the tower area. It took two years to restore, at a cost of about £500,000, and was reopened in 1987. (Taken by Dr Alan Pearson, Principal of Hild Bede College.)

Durham County Boy Scout Jamboree, 19–20 June 1948. It was held at The Park, Brancepeth Village, and was visited by the Chief Scout, Lord Rowallan, MC. 1,200 scouts attended. Five faces are identified in the central area: David Coates, Fred Schofield, John Alderson, Frank Bilton and Bob Stephenson.

Team members of Durham County Lawn Tennis Association, 1908. Back row, left to right: M.F. Watson, H. Widdas. Front row: T. Lumsden, H. Laws, C.A. Patterson and P. Widdas.

Durham City Cricket Club, league champions for the first time, 1907. Back row, left to right: A.B. Marreit (secretary), H. Sugden, C.R. Milam (professional), S.N. Veitch and three unknown. Middle row: F.E. Scott, C.Y. Adamson (captain), P.D. Robinson and A. Mangles. Front row: A. Featherstonhaugh and R. Newby. (Taken by W. Wilkinson.)

Durham City XI, cricket team 1902. Front row, seated, left to right: H. Hutton, J.J. Howe (captain), T. Hutton and C. Adamson. Second row: R. Rolfe, F. Scott and W.R. Wilson. Third row: J.Y. Bell, – Pennington, J. McCartan (in the white coat), T. Robinson and F. Adamson. Back row: T. Glendenning and T. Wison. (Taken by John Edis.)

Durham Prison Officers' cricket team, 1934. Back row, left to right: W. Moir (secretary), N. Rhodes, S. Aberdeen, T. Dove, A.L. Kitching, G. Turnbull, T. Kirk and W. Appleton. Front row: R.S. Alderson, Capt Chippington, J. Garr, C.O. Marjoram, J.H. Mills (captain), R. Wootton and J. Cross (scorer).

Durham City Cricket Club, league champions 1937. Back row, left to right: W. Phillips, J. Halliday, J.S. Eacott, T. Wilson, L. Linsley, T. Darling, G.W. Green, T. Barnfather, M. Bates. J. Cowan and J. Davidson. Front row: J.K. Glen, J.A. Adamson, C.L. Adamson, H.C. Ferens (captain), D. Glen, E.S. Cowell and J. Iley. (Taken by John Edis.)

Durham City Cricket Club, 1946. They were the second eleven league champions in 1947. Back row, left to right: T. Darling, K.L. Allan, E.H. Wilson, J.R. Coates, S. Holgate, J.G. Moody, J. Spikings and J. Mills. Middle row: J.E. Brockhill, T. Wilson, A. Bates (captain), J. Halliday and N. Fleming. Front row: M.S. Kyle, W.J. Jopling and J. Darling. (Taken by Daisy Edis.)

Mr Joseph Worthy (right), a trainer from Croxdale, with foot runner Wilf Fortune, c.1906. Joe was also a leading player with Durham City Rugby Club and was with the team that toured England in 1906. On that occasion, he was the only member to score a try. He was a contemporary of Bill Weaver, Harry Imrie (see page 59) and George Summerscale.

Frank Fleming of Durham City Harriers, pictured with his many trophies and prizes, August 1910. The 1901 census has a Frank Fleming listed at No. 78 Durham Road, Tudhoe, aged 12. He was still running for the club in 1914. The club was started on 24 November 1890 and had its formation meeting in Middleton's Cocoa Rooms, No. 23 Market Place, with the chair being occupied by Mr W. Deighton. They later held their meetings in the Criterion Hotel on the North Road side of Framwellgate Bridge.

St Cuthbert's Mission football team, *c*.1912. The mission room was at the head of Framwellgate, near the railway bridge (see page 26). It is now used as an office. On the reverse of the photograph is written, 'Left, John Bilton, became park keeper at Wharton Park.' (Taken by W. Wilkinson.)

Durham City AFC, nicknamed 'The Citizens', during the 1919–20 season. The players were Barnes, H. Patchett, Redpath, Dobson, A. Vincent, Avery, T. Davison, Cowell, Ferguson, Toward, Cousins, E. Young, Heather, Pattison and Thompson. *The Durham County Advertiser* announced that on 27 December 1918 a new Durham City Association Football Club had been formed.

Mackay's carpet factory football team, the winning team of the Durham County Amateur Cup match, 18 April 1937. The players were Hardman, Wood, Sharp, Wharton, Stocks, McArdle, Wardle, Patterson, Smith, Churchman and Cowan. Standing far right is Walter Shea.

Mackay's carpet factory football supporters, 18 April 1937. In the centre, holding the cup, is Arthur Stocks, captain and centre-half. They had just won the Durham County Amateur Cup, the first team in the city to secure the trophy since it was introduced in 1890. They had played Andrews House Rangers, members of the West Stanley and District League, at West Stanley Club, Murray Park, with a result of 3–0 to Mackay's.

Durham Wasps ice hockey team, 1948–49. Back row, left to right: John Smith, 'Gordie' Belmore, Bob Thompson, unknown, Jim Hall and unknown. Middle row: Ian Wardell, Butch (Bobby) Cartwright, G. Gibson, Joe Stephenson, Ron Sandcaster and Earl Carlson. Front row: Joe Bell and Bill Britt Jnr.

Two silver medals from the Crossgate House Academy (it stood over the road from St Margarets's Church). One is dated June 1835 and was awarded for the first-class prize at the annual examination. The other has no date and was awarded to Master Thomas Wetherall, a prize for geography. Both have a plain back.

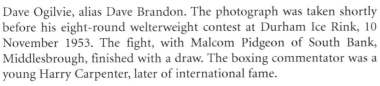

Dave Ogilvie, alias Dave Brandon. The photograph was taken shortly before his eight-round welterweight contest at Durham Ice Rink, 10 November 1953. The fight, with Malcom Pidgeon of South Bank, Middlesbrough, finished with a draw. The boxing commentator was a young Harry Carpenter, later of international fame.

A class from St Oswald's National School, Church Street, *c.*1890. The girl who is first left on the second row from the front is Margaret Horner, the daughter of Edward Horner of New Elvet. The school register has her entering in 1887 and leaving 1894 because she was then wanted at home. The school was erected in 1845, complete with a residence and garden for the master. It cost £1,500 and catered for about 500 children.

A football team from Castley's Bailey School, No. 9 Old Elvet, 1901. Back row, left to right: H. Holiday, Percy Manners, Lindsey Ogg, Bill Taylor, – Kelso and J. Landt Mawson. Front row: N. Slack, Joe Wood, Reggie Moyes, 'Fatty' Burton and N. Stokoe. (Taken by J.H. Castley.)

St Hilds' Demonstration School, known as the 'Dolly' Model School, Gilesgate, taken in the grounds of St Hild's College, *c.*1916. Teachers are, left to right: Miss Preston and Miss Hornsby. Back row, left to right: unknown, Norman Wilkinson, 'Home boy', Mary Gibson, Lesley Myers, Walter Robinson, Winnie Patterson, unknown, Reenie Potray, Jessie Harris and two unknowns. Second row: unknown, George Pearson, Dorothy Burnip, Percy Hodgson, – Peele, Dicky Peele, Evelyn Allan, Jimmy Allan and unknown. Front: unknown, 'Home boy', unknown, unknown, Alex Hush, Alice Allan, Geoffrey Caldcleugh, Harry Pounder and unknown. Walter Robinson, on the back row, was killed on 25 September 1944 while serving with the Royal Tank Regiment in the Netherlands.

Pupils from St Margaret's School, Margery Lane, Crossgate, 1900s. The children are performing their daily exercise in the schoolyard. The building was erected in 1859 and enlarged in 1889 to accommodate almost 500 children. The buildings on the top right have now been replaced by housing association apartments, reached by road from the top of Crossgate, opposite the former St Margaret's Hospital.

A rare interior photograph, showing pupils from Bluecoat School, Claypath, using the packing rooms formerly belonging to Henderson's Carpet Factory, Freeman's Place, 1912. This was during the school's reconstruction scheme of 1912–13, which was estimated to cost £3,800. Five classes are shown being taught in the one room. Sitting at his desk, on the left, is the headmaster, Fred Howarth (see page 123). They moved back to the old school in October 1913.

The Johnston Technical School, South Street, showing the sixth form and staff in the school yard, 1912. Standing third from the left is Mr P.G.S. Frogley, standing far right is Mr Sidney Whalley, and fourth from the right is Mr Marsden. (Taken by Speedy Photo Co., Durham.)

Performers of a French play at the Johnston Technical School, South Street, Christmas 1917. Standing, left to right: Miss Hirst, – Smith and Mr Sydney Whalley. Front: – Rose, unknown, – Robson, unknown and – Harrison.

Durham Girls' Grammar School staff, Providence Row, 1920s, taken outside the main entrance. The building was officially opened on 21 January 1914. The girls had previously attended the Johnston Technical School in South Street from 1901. The girls' school is now Durham Sixth Form Centre.

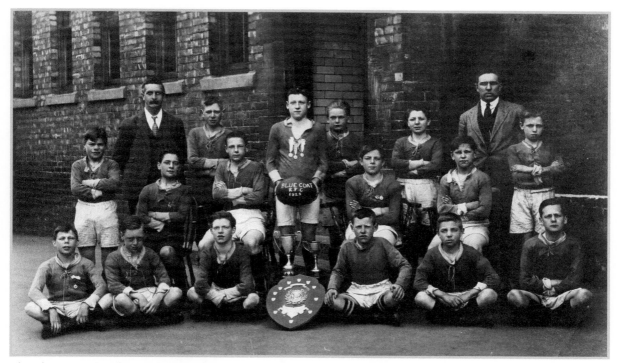

The Bluecoat School's rugby team, 1923. They are photographed outside the boys' entrance (see page 69). (Taken by The City Studio, Saddler Street.)

Pupils at work at Bow School (see page 151), Quarryheads Lane, 1938. The teacher was Miss Mildred M. Lodge. The photograph was taken the year Miss Lodge acquired the school, uniting it with Dunelm School, which she had founded at No. 37 South Street in September 1931.

St Margaret's School football team, 1945–46. Standing, left to right: Mr Thomas Brown (headmaster), P. Driver, C. Bird, J. Bartle, V. Carrol, D. Peacock and E. Hall. Seated: W. Forrester, F. Gibson, D. Lammin, J. Stewart and K. Brown.

The 'Dolly' Model in the late 1940s. The headmistress was Miss M.E. Aspinall. The fine stone building is now used by the university and is situated at the bottom of Gilesgate Bank, set back on the south side.

St Hild's School, *c*.1953. Back row, left to right: unknown, unknown, M. Allen, P. Martin, unknown, K. Hodgson, M. Rickaby, M. Bird and two unknown pupils. Second row: B. Swan, K. Donkin, unknown, unknown, J. Cairns, R. Banham, H. Cox, P. Akam and G. Conradi. Seated: unknown, R. Stevens, unknown, – Burdon, R. Adair, unknown, V. Barclay, unknown and B. Percy. Front: V. Plant, unknown, P. Coxon and H. Valentine.

A netball team from Whinney Hill School, taken outside the main entrance of the school, 1956–57. Left to right: unknown, Margaret Ellis, Sheila Hodgson, Dorothy Parkin and three unknown players. In the spring of 2010, the disused school was used as one of the film locations for the new TV series of *Inspector George Gently*.

Young sportsmen from Durham School, taken outside Poole House in the summer of 1934. The group includes, back row, left to right: P.C. Dunkley, D.J. Bottomley, J.S. Robinson, G.E. Greenwell, G.B. Willis (killed in action, Singapore, 14 February 1942), J.E. Linton and G.D. Spencer. Seated: C.F.L. Moffat (shot dead by an insane undergraduate in the quadrangle of University College, Oxford, 17 May 1940), H. Williams and D.L. Petrie (later killed while serving as a pilot officer with the RAF, 103 Squadron, 10 October 1941).

A fine view of young cricketers in the playing field of Durham School, 1860s. The oldest part of the school is Bellasis Cottage, the ivy-clad building on the left. This was altered in 1825 by the young architect Anthony Salvin and was lived in by Dr William Cooke, who taught medicine at the newly-founded university from 1832. His son William, inventor with Charles Wheatstone of the electric telegraph, experimented in the house. Salvin designed the new school buildings in 1844 when it moved here from Palace Green. (Taken by Thomas Heaviside.)

Bow School, Quarryheads Lane, 1900s. The first Bow School, opened in 1885 at 38 North Bailey, was originally called Bramwell's School after its founder, W.H. Bramwell. After its first year it was renamed Bow after the nearby church of St Mary le Bow. In 1889 the school moved to its present location.

Durham High School, left and, right St Chad's College, South Bailey, viewed from across the river in Church Street in the 1900s. The terraced gardens can be seen. This had been the second home (from 1886) of the school (the first was at No. 33 Claypath, which had opened in April 1884) before it was relocated to Leazes House, off Claypath, in 1912. (Taken by W. Wilkinson.)

An inside view of the first form, Durham High School, Leazes House, Claypath, *c.*1913. The building remained empty for a number of years after the school moved up to Farewell Hall in January 1968. In the 1970s some of the buildings were used by the university. It is now converted back into a family home and is reached from Leazes Place, off Claypath.

A bird's-eye view of Bluecoat School, taken from the roof of the former General Post Office, Claypath, *c.*1964. In the distance, behind the telegraph pole, is the newly-built Kingsgate Bridge, which had been opened in December 1963.

The Diocesan Training College for Females in the 1860s. The college was built by public subscription, aided by a government grant, to house 44 students, and was opened August 1858. At first it was only occupied by five students. It is now known as St Hild and St Bede College. The tower of St Giles's Church can be seen in the top right corner. (Taken by Thomas Heaviside.)

St Hild's College hockey team, 1906. In the centre is the principal, Revd Canon James Haworth, who lived in Grove House (see page 37), Gilesgate. He was born in Blackburn in 1853 and trained at St Mark's College, Chelsea, from 1872–73, then taught in London for two years before coming to Durham as a foundation scholar. Ordained at Farnham in 1879, he eventually came back to Durham in 1885 as Vice-Principal of St Hild's, becoming Principal from 1888–1910. He died on Easter Monday 1942. (Taken by John Edis.)

Bede Model School, Gilesgate, viewed from the grounds of Bede College, 1906. The school had officially opened on 20 February 1886 and closed in 1933. There had previously been a model school attached to Bede College from 1858, consisting of a school room in the college. The former school is now called Carter House.

The Diocesan Training College for Schoolmasters, showing the beginning of the newly-laid-out grounds in the 1870s. It had been established in 1841 and was later known as Bede College. It is now part of the united College of St Hild and St Bede. (Taken by R. Herbert.)

Bede College students, 1914–15. Many of these young men would have fought in World War One, and it is highly likely that some of their names appear on the college war memorial (see page 73).

A neat student room at No. 18 Norman Gallery, Durham Castle, University College, in 1890. The college was formed on the founding of the University of Durham in 1832. At that time the university had just one college. Durham Castle had been the home of the Bishops of Durham. Bishop William Van Mildert, one of the founders of the university, had intended the castle should be given to the college, it was transferred by Order in Council during the vacancy, following his death in 1836. Temporary accommodation for students was provided at Archdeacon's Inn, part of Cosin's Hall, on Palace Green, until University College moved into the castle in 1837. The castle keep, which had been in ruins, was restored for student accommodation.

Committee members of St Cuthbert's Society in the Cathedral cloisters during Easter term, 1893. Back row, left to right: E. Green, J.H. Sutcliffe and I.G. Ward. Middle row: N.N. Slade, W.F. Cullen and F.W. Shields. Front: H.F. Wilson and O. Jones.

The unattached students of Durham University, taken in the cloisters of the Cathedral during Easter term, 1893. These were students who lived in licensed lodgings and not in the college or halls. Most were older men as only those aged 23 or over were permitted to live out. They had no master or principal, no regular meeting, clubs or societies and no common room. They were only under the authority of the junior proctor.

An annual gathering of the Old Choristers' Association in the cloisters of Durham Cathedral, 1890s. Fifth from the right, seated in the second row, is Mr Arthur Pattison, who ran the well-known upholstery business at No. 20 Elvet Bridge. All appear to be wearing medals, which may indicate that they were attending a presentation. (Taken by John Edis.)

The staff and students of St Chad's College (established 1904), South Bailey, in 1928. During World War One part of the college (No. 17 North Bailey) was used by the 5th Durham Voluntary Aid Hospital. On the second row, seventh from the left, is Revd Stephen Richard Platt Moulsdale, Principal and Chaplain of St Chad's Hall and Vice-Principal of the university between 1934–36. (Taken by John Edis.)

Durham Colleges' Hockey Club, 1930–31. Back row, left to right: W.A. Lathaen, E.H. Jackson, J. Wright, W.J.C. Baldry and T.E. Sawyer. Front row: W. Chapman, H. Hope (honorary secretary), T. McGregor (captain), A. Roxby and P.L. O'Doherty. (Taken by John Edis.)

The Quadrangle, located to the rear of St John's College, at No.3 South Bailey, Durham, 1920s. This pleasant open space is now occupied by the William Leech Hall, officially opened on 25 June 1987. (Taken by R. Johnson, Gateshead.)

Students from St Hild's College in the 1920s, showing the head gardener, Mr Albert Richardson (the author's great-grandfather), teaching the art of preparing a garden at the student demonstration plot. This was located next to the college chapel, which was constructed by John Shepherd of Gilesgate and consecrated on 14 June 1913.

The student fire brigade belonging to St Hild's College, 1924–25. The college was founded in 1858 and was associated with the university from 1896. This was the year the first four Durham women graduates had their degrees conferred upon them. All were members of this college.

Durham Railway Station, ambulance class, photographed on the north-bound platform, 1914. A young lad can be seen on the stretcher. Many of these men would have later seen service in World War One. The wooden building behind the group remained well into the 1960s.

The 1926 committee of Durham City Working Men's Club, taken outside the Alms Houses, Palace Green, on the occasion of the club's silver jubilee 1901–26. Back row, left to right: W. Heighley (assistant. steward), H. Malton, J. Storey, J.W. Blagdon (steward), J.S. Grieveson and T.H. Elliot. Middle row: T. Coulthard, A.E. Chatterton (librarian), W. Hollis (secretary), Robert Spirit (president), J.F. Magee (treasurer), H.H. Fox and R.W.C. Modral. Front row: W. Gilbertson, F. Dixon and J.H. Chicken (door-keeper). (Taken by John Edis.)

The Olympia roller-skating rink, Freeman's Place, c.1909. The manager was Mr Vivian D'Alby. The rink was officially opened at 11am on Monday 27 December 1909 by the Mayor and Mayoress W.H. and Mrs Wood. It was in part of the building that had previously been used by Henderson's carpet factory.

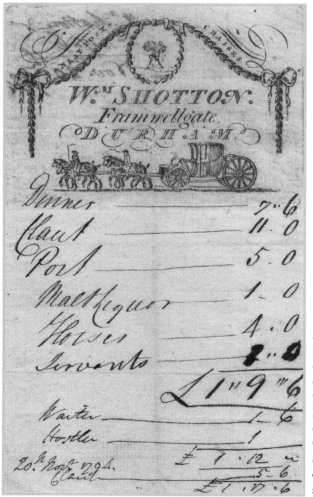

A rare bill-head from the Wheatsheaf Coaching Inn, Framwellgate, dated 20 November 1794. The total cost of the stay was £1 17s 6d, a substantial amount in those days. The owner was then William Shotton. When it was purchased by the Catholic Church in 1861 the large dining room was converted into a temporary chapel. The property eventually became part of St Godric's School. It has now been converted into apartments, along with the former brick-built school of 1898, which had previously been the site of the stables.

An outing from the Waterloo Hotel, No. 61 Old Elvet, 1920s. The building faced directly up New Elvet and was taken down in the early 1970s to make way for the New Elvet road bridge. Note the balcony, which is a smaller version of the one of its neighbour, The Royal County Hotel. (Taken by George Fillingham.)

The Spread Eagle, No. 34 Hallgarth Street, 1960s, taken from an album belonging to the City of Durham Trust. The hotel was situated at the bottom end of the street on the left-hand side, a little up from the forked junction.

The City Hotel, No. 84 New Elvet, *c.*1904, showing the landlord's name, H. Battensby. Note the figure in the first floor window on the left. In June 1962, during renovations by the owner Mr J.O. Luke, two ancient fireplaces were discovered, one thought to be from the Tudor period and the other Georgian. The present entrance is now on the left of the bay window.

The Dun Cow Hotel, No. 37 Old Elvet, *c.*1907. This is one of only a handful of Durham public houses still retaining its old world charm. A former landlord of 25 years was Tommy Wilson (see page 107). He was very popular with his customers.

The New Inn, Church Street Head, showing the landlord, Mr T. Derbyshire, and his wife, *c.*1910. Derbyshire had seen active service in the South African War with the 12th Royal Lancers, and in 1903 he joined the Durham County Constabulary, stationed at Jarrow, and later Shincliffe. He resigned in 1906 and then became landlord of the Station Hotel, Leamside before transferring to the New Inn. He died on 30 April 1914, aged 34.

A fine view of the bar of the New Inn, Church Street, 1900s. Note the period moustaches. Unfortunately it has been much altered inside to cater for the ever-increasing student population, but out of term-time it is virtually deserted.

Members of Durham City Working Men's Club photographed outside Nos. 49 and 50 Crossgate prior to an outing, 1920s. On the left a charabanc awaits its passengers, and on the right is an omnibus. Note the fine, cobbled road surface.

A group of men waiting at the bottom of Crossgate for the 'trip bus' for a day's outing in 1915. The business premises on the right are, left, R. Taylor, hairdresser, No. 78 Crossgate, and right, W. Lightfoot, fruiterer and florist, No. 1 North Road. (Taken by George Fillingham.)

The landlord and customers at the bar of the Castle Hotel, No. 18 Silver Street, *c*.1959. Left to right: unknown, Madge Jackson, Tom Giles, Isabel Bell, Mrs Giles and unknown. It is unusual to see a pint glass, as they traditionally only sold beer in half-pint glasses. The 'cellar' was a room behind the bar, cut into the solid rock of the hillside.

The Angel Inn, Crossgate, April 1957. The property dates from the 18th century. A period newspaper cutting from *The Newcastle Courant*, mentions a Mrs Wilkinson retiring from the inn around 1793, when the premises were listed as including a 'brew house'. It is now a popular establishment, especially with the younger generation.

The Duke of Wellington public house, Merry Oaks, 1930s. On the right of the main door is a framed timetable, possibly belonging to the United bus company. To the right of the hotel is the steep incline of Lowes Barn Bank, leading down to the bottom of Neville's Cross Bank, near the Stone Bridge Inn (see page 49).

The boys' bible class from St Nicholas' Church, 1890s. Two names on the reverse of the original photograph are: –Meade (second from the left, back row) and J. Mearis (eighth from the left, back row).

The choir of St Giles's Church, Gilesgate, 1880s. Taken by Joseph Chapelow who was a member of the church as well as a chemist, photographer and lemonade manufacturer. The group are photographed outside the vestry door on the south side of the church.

The junior branch of the Church of England Temperance Society, photographed outside the barracks (Vane Tempest Hall), *c*.1904. The girl, marked with the arrow (holding 'Cets 2') was Florence Greenwell, granddaughter of George Greenwell, founder of the well-known grocers at No. 33 Silver Street (see page 54). They have a banner with the letters 'C.E.T.S.' upon it. In the back row in the centre is Revd Francis Thomas, vicar of St Giles's Church.

Gilesgate Juvenile Jazz Band on the 'Duff Heap' Sunderland Road, 1930s. Front row, left to right: George Abbot Jnr, unknown, Ronnie Abbot, unknown, unknown, Joe Connell unknown. Second row: John George Wilkinson, George Abbott Snr, Harry Hogarth, unknown, Vince Tindale, Carter Watson, Anti (Anthony) Carr, Tommy Newton, Joe Connell Snr and unknown. Third row: Florrie Blacket, unknown, Margaret Scott, unknown, unknown, Esther Oliver, Winnie Wilkinson and three unknowns. Fourth row: two unknowns, Charlie McArdle, unknown, unknown, James Rayner, Otto Scott, Ralph Gleason and John Burke. Top row: unknown, Mima Horn, unknown, unknown, Harry Hopper and possibly Victor Lappage. The properties on the top right are the newly-built council houses of Musgrave Gardens. (Taken by George Fillingham.)

A group from St Nicholas's Boys' Club, No. 96 Claypath, c.1953. Three of the adult helpers in the back row, left to right, are Joe Robinson, Mr W.L. Wilson and Maurice Andrewartha (a University College student). The lad in the front row has a 'must-have' item for all young boys at the time, a catapult. The club was founded in 1933 and catered for boys from the age of eight to 16. Its main aim was to train boys in Christian ways.

St Nicholas's Boys' Club at Capenwray Hall, Carnforth, Lancashire, 1948. Back row, left to right: J. Cleasby and Lung Wong. Middle row: B. Elliot, B. Herring, D. Fox, A. Simpson and A. Baldwin. Front row: S. Baldwin, P. Kelly (a relative of the author), J. Stewart and R. Baldwin.

Members of Vane Tempest Hall (now Gilesgate Community Association) tennis club, *c.*1950. Back row, left to right: unknown, A. Stephenson, unknown, unknown, S. Dixon, W. Morrow, unknown and J. Stewart. Front row: S. Francis, V. Reed, Theresa Scott, Eileen Glenton and unknown.

St Nicholas's Scout troop in Bailes' Yard, Walkergate, *c.*1925. The old building on the right behind the group was their meeting place. Back row, standing, left to right: unknown, Ernie Kirk, Lesley Bell, Mr Druitt, Tommy Collins, Bill Bradley, Harry Pounder and Philip Proctor. Second row, left to right: George Kirk, unknown, Walter Tilly, John Vasey, Norman Robinson, Harry Davis, Mr Davis, Septimus Robinson, Arthur Eales, Edwin Robinson, unknown and Arthur Rickaby. Front ends, left: unknown and Matty Eccles.

A group of boys from the 4th Durham Scouts outside St Giles's Church, *c.*1947. Back row, left to right: unknown, and George McGregor. Third row: unknown, George Parry, David Coates, Frank Bilton, Bill Bailey and Arthur Wales. Second row: Tom Grey, unknown, unknown, Brian Stidwell and Peter Robinson. Front row: Billy Griffiths, unknown, Jimmy Harris, George Grey and – Wilkinson. (Taken by J.C. Bailey of Langley Moor.)

Members of St Oswald's Guides, Brownies and Sea Rangers, photographed in the garden of St Oswald's vicarage, Church Street in 1949. Back row: Dorothy Shea, Audrey Stobbs, Doreen Maddison, June McIntrye, Kathleen Surtees, Sheila Brown, Margaret Pawson, Jean Urquhart, Stephanie Davies and Elsa Bunting. Third row: Audrey McIntyre, Maureen Hogg, Moira Keegan, Eleanor Todd, unknown, Pat Waites, Kathleen Horn, Ruby Spikings, Kathleen Hogg, Margaret Wales, Margaret Almond, Mary Allen, Shelia Mitchinson, Leticia (Trish) Melville and Win Slater. Second row: Ethel Dunn, Marie Petrie, Margaret Morris, Miss Gardiner, Mrs Theresa Morse, Miss Freda Davies, Gladys Parlett, Anne Dodds, Elsie Loftus and A. Corner. Front row: - Thompson, unknown, Betty Loftus, Sheila Hodgson, unknown, Pat Lancaster, unknown, unknown, Win Loftus and two unknowns. The photograph was taken as a farewell gift for Mrs Morse, wife of the vicar, Revd Hilary Morse, who was moving to Carlisle.

The North Durham Hunt, 1890s. The hunt was established in 1872, when the Durham County Hounds were divided between Mr Harvey and Mr Anthony Lax Maynard of Newton Hall. The latter became the first master of the NDH and resigned in 1882 due to age. It was dissolved in 1943.

Members of the Sir G.B. Cumming's Lodge, RAOB, 1914–18. Seated at the front left is Edward Cummings, blacksmith from Malvern Terrace, Sherburn Road. He later moved over the road to Malvern Villas. Three members are pictured wearing World War One army uniforms. The uniforms are, left to right: Durham Light Infantry, Royal Field Artillery and Northumberland Fusiliers. The Royal Antediluvian Order of Buffaloes, familiarly know as 'The Buffs', is a social and charitable organisation dating back to the 1820s. During World War One it funded ambulances on the front line and ran orphanages and convalescent homes. (Taken by The City Studio, Saddler Street.)

A ladies' exercise class held in St Margaret's Institute, Crossgate, 1930s. The building was demolished around 1974, and the site is now occupied by housing association apartments. (Taken by George Fillingham.)

A gathering of Old Girls and their babies, photographed for a Christmas reunion at Whinney Hill School, December 1957. In the centre is Miss Barker, playing the role of Father Christmas, and two rows above her, to the left, is headmistress Miss Viola Flemming.

St Giles's Young Wives in January 1957. The vicar was then Canon Jack Norwood. Husbands and friends of the Young Wives Club were entertained by members at the club's annual party, which was held in the church hall (now the site of St Giles's Filling Station). After supper there was crazy whist, dancing and games. Back row, left to right: Mr Davies, unknown, Albert Tulip, Cliff Morgan, unknown, unknown, Mrs Pease, John Scarr and Norman Jennings. Third row: Mr Wilson, Mayna Owens, Les Oates, Arthur Dixon, unknown, Mr Tompson, Mrs Tulip, Miss Rogers, Mrs Fowler, Mrs Morgan, Norman Watson, George Stephenson, Jim Moody and Mr Hutchinson. Second row: Maisie Oates, Gladys Dixon, Jean Morgan, unknown, Ellen Hutchinson, Mrs Norwood, Canon Jack Norwood, Alice Whitfield, Winnie Whitfield, Rena Jennings and Winnie Thompson. Front row: Doris Moody, Mrs Wilson, unknown, Nancy Watson, Win Thompson, Betty Brown and Lily Scarr.

Staff and guests from Neville's Cross High School, June 1957. The occasion was the annual prize-giving ceremony, held at the Miners' Hall, Red Hill. The Principal, Mrs E. Hunter, told parents that 'Discipline in the home is essential, and children should always be sent to bed at a suitable time with regularity, otherwise they appear at school the next day lethargic and stupid.' (*The Durham County Advertiser*)

Durham railwaymen at the North Road Station, January 1951. This group, along with others, had been engaged in a quiz for potential engine drivers, playing against a team from Consett at Durham City.

Steam engine No. 64931, pictured at Belmont Junction on Tuesday 5 August 1952. It was a member of Class J39, the most numerous of Sir Nigel Gresley's locomotive designs for the LNER. Built in 1937, it was cut up in 1961 as British Rail converted to diesel trains. The line on the right branched off to Gilesgate Goods Station, now a Travelodge and restaurant. (Taken by D.J. Chadwick.)

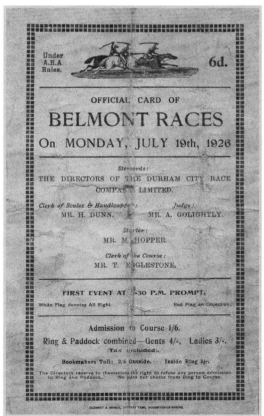

A rare horse-racing programme for Belmont Races, Monday 19 July 1926. The course was situated near the present Cheveley Park shopping centre. The races were managed by the directors of The Durham City Race Company Ltd.

The yard of the Grange Iron Works, Carrville, 1900s. Parts are being loaded onto NER wagons. A railway siding came into the works' yard from the Gilesgate Goods line, linking up to the Leamside line. (Taken by John Edis.)

A performance of *Othello* by members of the men's drama group belonging to West Rainton Social Service Centre in March 1937. The event was organised by Miss Margot Daniels.

On the back of the original postcard was written, 'An open-topped motor bus, at one of the stopping places near the high church gate, West Rainton,' *c*.1913. The bus has a Sunderland destination plate, and the registration number: AH 0136.

The fine, stone-built rectory of St Mary's Church, West Rainton, *c*.1914, showing two young ladies with their dog in the garden. It is now a private residence, situated at the east end of the village, across the A690 road.

Mr Alex Welsh, then working for the Rural District Council, with his horse and cart, emptying the ash closets at Drapers' Row, West Rainton, in the late 1920s. In the background is Leamside School.

The new foot-bridge crossing the Wear to the ruins of Finchale Priory *c*.1938. For many years a toll was paid to cross this bridge. Finchale is recorded as early as AD 792, when it was the site of a Synod for the Northumbrian Church. A further two meetings were held here in, AD 798 and AD 810, which suggests it was an important place long before the Benedictine monks from Durham began building the priory here, around 1237.

Finchale Abbey, August 1960. The building was being constructed under the guidance of 'Icy Smith' (Mr J.F.J. Smith, who founded Durham Ice Rink), on the right with hat. It was intended to become a chapel and shrine to the memory of St Godric, but the work was never completed as it was carried out without planning permission.

The east corner of the north aisle of St Lawrence's Church, Pittington, in the 1900s, showing a fine carved oak lectern. It has an inscription on brass attached to the base which reads: 'This lectern is given in dear remembrance of our father Henry John Baker Baker of Elmore. Born, June 29 1822, Died, January 28 1871.' The memorial tablet on the wall was to Captain George Conyers Baker Baker, 60th Rifles, of Elemore Hall. He died on 11 June 1892 and is buried at Mandalay, upper Burma. (Taken by W. Wilkinson.)

The frontage of Piper's first shop, Front Street, Low Pittington, 1920s. The young lad on the left is Charlie Piper with his sisters, Evelyn (with glasses) and Elizabeth. The two without cycles are unknown. The shop was destroyed by a fire on the afternoon of 24 January 1934.

An ancient wooden shovel found when old mine workings were broken into at Frankland Finchale Colliery in the 1930s. The date, 1500, had been chalked on by the finder.

An inside view of Alf Piper's grocer's shop, Front Street, Low Pittington, c.1930. Left to right: Evelyn Piper, Charlie Piper (see page 79) and mother Elizabeth Piper. It was a typical well-stocked shop of the period that sold everything needed around the home.

Alf Piper, grocer and provision merchant, High Pittington (situated at the crossroads), 1930s. This was his new shop, having moved up here from Low Pittington. The business was sold to the Pittington Co-operative Society in 1946 when Alf retired. For many years after this area was known as 'Piper's Corner'.

Littletown's 1925 cricket team, photographed outside Littletown House, then the home of the colliery manager. Back row, left to right: – Robinson, J. Fisk, W. Smith and G. Lloyd. Third row: S. Last, P. Judd, G. Broughton, J. Burt, E. Last and Jim Burt. Front row: Tom Elliot and W. Adamson. The umpire on the right is Sam Last. Non-players, left to right, are Sam Blunt, Joe Jenkins, J. Miller, unknown, unknown, G. Barnfather, W. Neave, – Robinson and unknown. Front, seated left to right, are W. Hunter, Mr Hornsby (colliery manager) and W. Hamilton (scorer).

Three generations of the Simpson family, Littletown's 'bonesetters'. Left to right: William (1870s), Thomas (1890s) and John (1920s). There are many references throughout the Durham area to the Simpsons fixing broken limbs, especially those of the miners.

The gamekeepers' cottages, Elemore Hall Woods, near Littletown, 1930s. The first cottage on the left was then lived in by Mr Dingle, and the other was occupied by Tom Harland.

Littletown School Group, *c*.1938. The teacher was Miss Hinds. Back row, left to right: L. Tate, Joan Wilkes, Sheila Dodd, Hilda Wild, Irene Smith, Jim Harper and Denis Law. Middle row: Elizabeth Simpson, Bill Blacklock, Harry Rutter, Ann Jones, Iris Goodchild, Ben Simpson, Ken Hall, Norman Hopper and Chris Carman. No names are recorded for the front row.

Sherburn Hill Colliery Girls' School, group 1, 1890s. The area was well populated at this time, with its long rows of pit cottages both on the north and south sides of the hill. These became squalid and damaged by mining subsidence. They were all eventually demolished as new council houses were constructed at Sherburn Village and at the 'Busty', the area on the north side of the hill.

The first 'Songster Brigade', Sherburn Hill Salvation Army, taken outside their former hall *c*.1924. Back row, left to right: N. Smith, J. Crawford, T. Suggett, B. Errington, R. Crawford, T. Jarvis, L. Joicey, V. Harper, J. Holman and G. Stead. Middle row: D. Stones, M. Errington, Mrs Cowley, Mrs Carroll, A. Patterson, Mrs Punton, Mrs Kell, Mrs McDonald and B.M. Kell. Front row: R. Patterson, T. Raine, G. Cowley, Capt Twine, Lieut Carr, Mr Ord and E. Peachey.

The Singing Company and Mandolin Band, Sherburn Hill Salvation Army, 1944. Back row, left to right: J. Dixon, K. Raine, C. Carman, Mrs Adj Reynolds, B. Oxley, A. Wilkinson and S. Meredith. Middle row: M. McDonald, D. McDonald, E. Kell, S. Kell, J. Robertson, J. Usher, E. Dixon, J. Luke and E. Craggs. Front row: W. Kell, O. Meredith, D. Turnbull, Mrs D. Punton (leader), S. Reynolds, H. Dixon and A. Heaton.

The coal-tipple, Sherburn Hill Colliery, *c.*1959. This was the contraption that carried the coal tubs to be emptied. The notice on the right warns people not to travel on the creeper while it is in motion. Note the upturned sleeper carrier on the left. (Taken by Billy Longstaff of Sherburn Village.)

The lamp-room, Sherburn Hill Colliery, *c.*1960. These common lamps now command high prices of between £70–90. After the mines closed many were thrown down the shaft. (Taken by Billy Longstaff.)

An aerial view of High House Farm, Sherburn Hill, 1950s. This farm was one of two belonging to the Co-operative Society. On the right was the field used by Sherburn Hill United football club. The goal posts can be seen.

Potato picking at High House Farm, Sherburn Hill, 1954. Driving the tractor is Margaret Youngman, the farmer's daughter. This was once a popular school holiday in October called, 'Potato Picking Week', an opportunity for mothers and their children to earn a few shillings plus a bucket of 'spuds' each day.

Mr Arthur Hindmarch, a farm hand at High House Farm, Sherburn Hill, 1954. He is seen making straw batons, used to line the potato pits for storing the crop over the winter months. Part of the pit-heap of Sherburn Hill colliery is visible in the background.

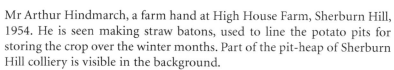

Mr John Athey Youngman, farm manager, thatching a stack at High House Farm, Sherburn Hill, 1950s. He was born at Kirkley Mill, Northumberland, and came to be foreman at Carr's Farm, South Hetton, in 1919. In May 1939 he took the job as farm manager at High House Farm, and in 1945 he moved to manage Hallgarth Farm, Pittington. After moving back to manage High House in 1949, he retired to Carrville in 1958.

Thomas Hope, photographed here in his later years in the 1870s. Mr Hope was responsible for building the row of 15 houses in Sherburn Village during the 1860s, which was aptly named Hope Street. The street still stands, although some of the houses were demolished for development several years ago. Hope Street today starts at No. 6 and ends at No. 11. (Taken by Thomas Heaviside.)

Sherburn Colliery Primitive Methodist Chapel, Sherburn Village, *c.*1908. The chapel was built to seat 150 people in 1862 at a cost of around £200. It was at the west end of the village, on the right side of the road as you entered from Durham. Records held at Durham County Hall suggest its closure around 1953. The site is now partly occupied by Smiths Close.

The through-road of Sherburn Village looking east towards Sherburn Hill, 1920s. Until the 19th century Sherburn was a farming village. With the arrival of the Industrial Revolution came the sinking of coal mines to provide fuel for industries and railways. By the 1930s the two collieries, Sherburn House and Lady Durham, were shut, and with the closing of neighbouring collieries in the 1960s the railway lines and stations also became redundant.

An old cottage attached to the stables of Sherburn Hall, Sherburn Village, 1900s. The stone frontage of the building was later rendered and white-washed (see page 190). It is now demolished, and the land is occupied by the working men's club car park.

Sherburn Village, *c.*1960. Left to right: the old cottage, originally connected to the stable block of Sherburn Hall; the working men's club, opened in 1959; and Satterley's lock-up. They sold hardware around the villages from a covered trailer (pictured). Satterley's premises are now used as a health and beauty salon. (Taken by Billy Longstaff)

A pageant by members of Sherburn Village British Legion women's section on 18 July 1941. Note the women wearing Women's Land Army outfits on the left, and third on the right is a lady with NAAFI (Navy, Army and Air Force Institutes) on her headwear.

Sherburn Hill Salvation Army at one of their Monday night open-air meetings in Sherburn Village, near the crossroads, June 1951. The army are still very active within the local communities.

Sherburn Village crossroads, looking towards the outbuildings of Hall Farm, *c.*1960. The last two families to live there were the Dobsons and finally the Lawsons. The area of the outbuildings are now occupied by houses, part of Peart Close. (Taken by Billy Longstaff.)

A decorated rolley belonging to Bowburn and Coxhoe Co-operative Store at Bowburn Show, *c.*1913. The display consists of a tailor's dummy and a Singer table sewing machine from the drapery department. They were awarded second prize for their effort. (Taken by George Fillingham.)

Miners from Bowburn Colliery in the early 1960s prior to their descent into the mine. The first coal was brought up in October 1908, and the pit closed in July 1967. The author's grandfather, Jimmy Savage, was banksman here for over 30 years. He passed on the tubs of coal as they were brought to the surface to the pair of checkweighmen (one each appointed by the owners and the union) The checkweighman recorded their agreed weight and sent empty tubs in their place down the shaft.

The ruins of Coxhoe Hall, *c.*1950. Built *c.*1725, it was the birthplace of Elizabeth Barrett (1806), the poet who went on to marry Robert Browning. In September 1938 it ceased to be a family home when it was bought by the East Hetton Colliery Co. At the beginning of World War Two it was requisitioned by the Government for troops. Near the end of the war Italian prisoners were moved in, followed by Germans. After the war it fell into a run-down state and squatters moved in. Mining subsidence had caused structural damage, and in August 1952 it was pulled down.

The opening of Coxhoe Social and Literary Institute by John Wilson MP, 19 November 1910. It was converted from four small cottages, which stood on the site where the present war memorial stands. The new institute consisted of a large billiard and snooker room, with a room at each end for reading and games.

The old blacksmith shop in Coxhoe, 1900s. The end cottage on the left has a barber's pole outside. The area to the right is now partly occupied by Coxhoe Working Men's Club.

The old mill at Coxhoe, 1900s. At the time of the photograph it was run by George Turnbull. It ceased to be water-powered during his tenancy when the mechanism broke down. The squire, John Wood of Coxhoe Hall, decided it would be difficult to fix and installed a petrol engine in its place. The mill was taken down in 1965.

Members of Coxhoe Primitive Methodist Church, Church Street, 1916, taken at the time of their 50th anniversary. The foundation stone was laid in 1865, and the church opened a year later. It cost £355 and could seat about 400 people. It finally closed in 1964 and is now part of Gatenby's Store.

The 12th-century St Helen's Church, Kelloe, 1890s. This fine building lies east of the present village, surrounded by trees. It is all that is left of the deserted mediaeval settlement of Church Kelloe.

The ancient cross inside St Helen's Church, Kelloe, 1930s. This early 12th-century Norman sandstone cross is believed to have been sculpted and brought here from France. It depicts scenes featuring St Helen, mother of the first Christian Roman Emperor, Constantine. It was found in six pieces, embedded into the chancel wall, during restoration work in 1858. In 1984 the cross spent three months on display at the Hayward Gallery, London, along with other priceless treasures from around the world.

Village children gather outside the Wesleyan Chapel, Kelloe, 1900s. The village derives its name from Caluh Law, meaning 'Bare Hill', and was a settlement during the Bronze Age.

The disused Crow Trees Colliery, Quarrington Hill, 1950s. Opened in 1825, it first closed in 1857 before being reopened later. It closed again in 1877, was reopened, and closed permanently in 1897.

The colliery houses of South View, Quarrington Hill, 1900s. The huge pit heaps in the background look like mountains. These belonged to the East Hetton Colliery.

Front Street, Quarrington Hill, 1920s. On the main street is the Primitive Methodist chapel, erected in 1886, at a cost of £400, to seat almost 300 worshippers. On the extreme right is part of the pub sign belonging to The Black Boy Inn.

Mr Joseph Lumsden Gatenby, photographed outside his wireless and gramophone shop at Steetley Terrace, Quarrington Hill, 1930s. The business is still very active in the old mining villages east of the city.

The former St Paul's Church, Quarrington Hill, 1900s. It was constructed for the inhabitants of Quarrington Hill and Cassop. The stones used in its construction were said to have been transported by William Smith, innkeeper of the Half Moon Inn, Quarrington Hill, as he was the only villager to own a heavy cart to make this possible. It was closed during the 1980s. The churchyard is still used for burials.

An interior view of St Paul's Church, Quarrington Hill, 1900s. It was consecrated in 1868, and it was unfortunately taken down in 1993. Oil lamps, on the left of the picture, were then used in the church.

An outdoor service held at Burn Hall, near Croxdale, late 1920s. The hall was at this time occupied by St Joseph's College, Junior Seminary of the Catholic Order of Missionaries. It had been purchased by them in 1926. The Victorian Grade II listed conservatory still survives, built *c*.1900, and the hall has now been converted into private apartments.

A grand North Eastern Railway engine with the number 661, one of the NER's 398-Class of fast freight locos, stopped at Croxdale, 1890s. A total of 325 were built from 1871, about half by their own workshops at Gateshead, Darlington and York, and the rest by contractors.

The top of the stone arch from the walk-way being constructed under the new Croxdale Bridge, 29 May 1926. The bridge work was necessary because the Durham to Darlington Road was being widened. (Taken by John Edis.)

St Bartholomew's Church, Croxdale, *c*.1910. It was built in 1843 by the Salvin family in exchange for the old church (see page 202). It was enlarged in 1878 by the addition of a chancel and a new nave on the north side of the original building. The cottage on the left was then occupied by the local policeman – note the police badge above its front door. The property was removed when the Durham to Darlington Road was widened between 1924–26. The shingled spire was removed sometime around 1960.

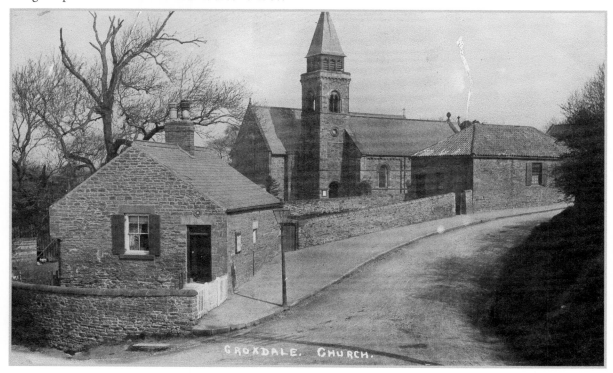

The 12th-century Grade I listed chapel, dedicated to St Bartholomew, 1890s. Now redundant, it stands in the grounds next to Croxdale Hall. It was in use as a chapel of ease to St Oswald's, Elvet, until the new parish church of St Bartholomew was built by the Salvin family in 1843. Each September the building is accessible to the public on Heritage Open Days.

An interior view of Croxdale Hall Chapel, 1900s. This Gothic-style Roman Catholic chapel is situated in the north wing of the hall. It was designed by James Wyatt around 1807 for the Salvin family, who had occupied the estate since 1402. During World War Two the hall was used as a military hospital, and was subsequently a maternity home until about 1952. It has now reverted back into the family home of the Salvins.

Quarry Hill House, Brancepeth Village, *c.*1907. The building was an early 17th-century structure, which had been much altered and extended in the late 19th century. For many years it has been the home of the Nicholson family, long associated with Vaux Breweries. (Taken by H. Coates.)

A group of young boys fixing a cycle puncture at Brancepeth Village, August 1963. The building on the left is the former village school. At the time of the photograph, plans were being drawn up to make the area a student village for the University of Durham.

Looking down Browney Lane, Meadowfield, *c.*1907. At the bottom of the street was the colliery and rows of pit cottages. The mine was opened 1871 and closed July 1938. (Taken by H. Coates.)

One half of a stereo view labelled 'Brandon Colliery', showing children playing in a back lane, 1890s. These dwellings were typical of the pit villages around the city.

The rear view of a pit cottage at Brandon Colliery, decorated for the coronation of King George V and Queen Mary, 22 June 1911. The original postcard was labelled 'Auntie Nan's House.'

Langley Moor Football Club, winners of Brandon Nursing and the Deerness Nursing Cups 1913–14. Back row, left to right: Dr Sinclair, T. Tierney, R. Stobbs, J. Staples, G. Ross, W. Stobbs, T. Turnbull (chairman), W. Robertshaw, J. Mulhall, R. Rowell and J. Davies. Third row: N. Winter, W. Emery, J. Ferguson, T. Lawson, D. Oakley, J. Moffitt, J. Fenwick, W. Fishwick and R. Smith (secretary). Second row: Dr Wilson (president), G. Rycroft, F. Bowes, E. Hopper (captain), J. Ferguson (vice-captain), R.A. Foster, T. Warriner and Mrs Wilson. Front row: J. Griffiths, E. Nelson, the Brandon and Deerness Cups, J. Welsh, F. Greenwell and J. Mossop.

A Daimler bus with 'No. 1' painted on the side, belonging to John Bassey, Langley Moor, *c.*1930. The driver and conductor, with passengers on board, find time to pose for a photograph. The destination plate reads 'New Brancepeth'.

The grounds staff working in Holliday Park, Langley Moor, 1920s. The drive led to a large 17-roomed house called Langley Grove, at one time occupied by the North Brancepeth Coal Company's manager, Mr Martin Holliday. In 1919 he gave the park to Brandon Byshottles District Council 'to be kept always as an open space to be used and enjoyed by the public'.

Edward Wilkinson, landlord of the Coach and Horses, Pity Me, *c.*1904, photographed driving his 1903 French-made 'De Dion'. It had a 698cc engine and a two-speed gearbox. Edward was the son of a Hexham bowler-hat manufacturer.

An aerial view of Nelson's removal business on the Lanchester Road, opposite Earls House Hospital, 1970s. The founder of the business George Robert Savage Nelson is a relative of the author. A new luxurious bungalow now stands in the field where the caravan is on the left. The site was once occupied by Tunstall House.

Coroner John Graham, left, and his second wife, Ellen, in the trap pulled by 'White Heather', *c.*1907. They are outside the 'Well House', Findon Cottage, which is situated on the left-hand side of the road, along a track before you reach Findon Hill, Sacriston. The Dales pony was bought in Newcastle by the coroner and was previously called 'Little Prim'.

Two coal miners from Sacriston, 1900s after returning home from the colliery, before the days of the pit baths. Durham County Record Office have a copy of this postcard which is labelled Birtley. The original is in the author's collection and has Sacriston written on the reverse.

Moseley Banks waterfall on the River Browney, near Aldin Grange, *c*.1911. On the left a young man prepares himself for a dip, to the amusement of his friends on the opposite bank.

The steam locomotive, No.1, owned by Ferens and Love, Cornsay Colliery, *c*.1910. The engine driver and fireman are self-consciously posing for the camera. (Taken by H. Coates.)

Laying of a foundation stone for No. 4 Aged Miners' Homes, Bearpark, *c*.1930. This was laid on behalf of Bearpark Working Men's Club and Institute by Joseph Holmes Esq. The homes were officially opened in 1931 by Sir John Fry, Bart.

Bearpark Colliery,1930s. It was sunk in 1872 and closed on 6 April 1984. On the left in front of the building are stacks of wooden pit-props for supporting the roof of the mine below ground.

The aerial flight at Bearpark Colliery, 1930s. This carried the waste material from the mine to nearby pit heaps. On the left are huge tree trunks, stacked ready to be cut for pit props for use underground.

Bearpark Colliery Band, early 1920s. The band was founded in 1920 by Mr I. Owens. For more information on the village see *A Mining World; The Story of Bearpark* by Douglas Pocock, 1985.

The ruins of Bearpark Priory in the 1900s. Also called Beaurepaire (the beautiful retreat), it originally consisted of 100 acres and was given by Gilbert de la Lay of Witton in 1154. This eventually grew to about 1,300 acres and belonged to the Abbey Church at Durham. It was the summer retreat for the Prior of Durham and his Benedictine Monks. (Taken by W. Wilkinson.)

The Primitive Methodist Chapel, Bearpark Colliery Road, Bearpark, 1900s. It was opened in 1884 to seat 360 people, and it is now empty after many years of being used by an organ builder. (Taken by F.W. Leeming, Ushaw Moor.)

Harvest festival decorations at the Primitive Methodist Chapel, Bearpark, 1900s. The produce would have been grown by the local miners in their allotment gardens.

The staff from Bearpark coke-works, 27 September 1907. The works had 50 Simon Carves by-product recovery ovens, which produced benzol oil, ammonia and coal-tar from the coal. In the first years of steam locomotives, coke was the normal fuel.

The doctor's house and surgery, Kelvin House, Nos. 1 and 2 Victor Terrace, Bearpark, *c.*1910. The house is still used and is now part of the Dunelm practice. The frontage remains the same, with its fine canopy and columns.

Ushaw Moor branch of the New Brancepeth Co-operative Store, situated on the Durham Road, showing its 18 members of staff *c.*1914. The name 'Ushaw' means 'the Wolf's Wood'.

Pearson's shop, near Ushaw College, 1900s. This was the local haunt for students from the seminary and was run by Mrs Frances Pearson, seen to the left of the group.

The Ushaw jubilee bonfire in 1935, celebrating King George V and Queen Mary's 25 years on the throne. Its was 62ft high, had a circumference of 134ft and consisted of about 400 tons of wood. Ushaw College can be seen to the left in the background.

The old mill in the grounds of Ushaw College, damaged beyond repair in a severe gale of 1853. In 1884 it was lowered to make an agricultural silo. It is famed as the mill in which Alderman Featonby Gribble was immured during the famous 'Wharton Election', held in the city in 1802. He had been an open supporter of Wharton, and the opposition had kidnapped him and locked him in the old mill until after the election.

St Catherine's Church, New Brancepeth, *c.*1906. The church was consecrated, 11 September 1890. It was destroyed by fire, 4 July 1942 when two youths had entered the vestry and lit candles. A decorator is seen on his ladder to the left of the porch.

Interior St. Catherine's Church, New Brancepeth. 3816

The interior of St Catherine's Church, New Brancepeth, 1920s. The church was a chapel of ease to St John the Evangelist, Meadowfield. Today the site of the church has reverted back to farm land. (Taken by R. Johnson and Son, Gateshead.)

Miners seeking coal near Deerness during the minimum wage strike, which occurred, 1 March 1912. It lasted until 26 March, when the Wage Act was passed.

A staff photograph of Esh Co-operative Society Ltd (Provision Dealers), 1900s. A heavy wagon-load, complete with a chain-horse to help with the hills, can be seen. The chap behind the wagon on the footpath has a wooden peg-leg.

The old village cross (Grade II listed), Esh, 1900s. Whellan's Directory of Co. Durham, 1856, records the inscription 'IHS' on the cross and its completion date as 1687. It is believed to stand on the site of an earlier mediaeval structure. It was restored in 1999 by David Edwick, a stonemason from Hexham. The ornate gate piers, relocated here in 1857, belonged to the former ancient hall, which had long been the home of the De Eshes. The mansion was taken down in 1857, and the stone was used to build the present Esh Hall Farm.

St Michael the Archangel's Church, Old Esh, viewed from near Hall Road *c.*1908. The earliest known reference to the church is in a charter by Bishop Beck in 1283. (Taken by T.W.)

An inside view of St Michael's Church, Esh, 1900s. 'The Parish Church is a small stone structure, dedicated to St Michael, and occupies the site of a chapel of very ancient date. An inscription upon a stone in the north wall states that it was rebuilt in 1770. It was again restored in 1850, and in 1889 improvements were made at a cost of £200. The church consists of nave, chancel and south transept, and a neat porch, added in 1884 by public subscription, to the memory of Revd Dr Edward Lee, the vicar here for 10 years, who died on 6 March 1884. The bell bears the inscription 'Maria Gratiana, 1695.' (From *History, Topography and Directory of Durham*, Whellan, London, 1894.)

Temperance Cottage, on the left side of the road, as you approach Esh Winning from Durham, between Broadgate and East Flass Farms, *c.*1907. There is an old couple at the front and a young child at the gate-post. (Taken by F.W. Leaming.)

A rare underground view of a coal seam in Esh Pit, *c.*1912. The mine was divided between the north and south sides. The north was accessed by a drift and the south had a shaft. The colliery was sunk in 1856 and closed in 1968. The young lad on the left has a cigarette in his mouth. Note the rich coal seam and the small area to work in. (Taken by George Gilford, No. 57 Durham Road, Esh Winning.)

Esh Winning Rangers AFC, season 1908–09. The village of Esh Winning was built in the 19th century to provide homes for local coal miners. The name Esh derives from the nearby Esh Village, meaning 'ash', as in the tree. 'Winning' describes the finding, or winning, of coal.

The Cycle Parade, Waterhouses, *c*.1905. Some are wearing their Boys' Brigade uniforms, and the central character is seated on a donkey. Many pit villages had these parades, sometimes to help a needy family but mainly to raise funds for local charities.

St Joseph's Catholic Church and Presbytery, Ushaw Moor, *c*.1931. The foundation stone was laid by Bishop Joseph Thorman, 19 June 1930, and the building was officially opened 21 April 1931. The bell for the new building was given by the people of Ballingarry, south-east Tipperary. After seven years the church was free of debt and on 17 May 1938 Bishop McCormack performed the ceremony of consecration.

Looking towards the altar of St Joseph's Church, Ushaw Moor, *c*.1931. The first St Joseph's Roman Catholic Church was established in Ushaw Moor and opened on 19 December 1909. It was a corrugated iron structure and cost £474.

The brick and tile works of Cornsay Colliery, *c.*1903. The coal mine yielded a splendid quality of fireclay (seggar) and blue stone, ideal for the brick, tile and sanitary pipe industries. Behind the works are the houses of Stable Street, Office Street, Liddle Street, Chadwick Street and High Street, all now demolished. A tree plantation occupies some of the works' site today.

Commercial Street, the main road through the village of Cornsay Colliery, *c.*1910. This was the only privately-owned row out of 13 streets making up the village, the rest being colliery-owned houses. (Taken by H. Coates.)

Shaft sinkers at Cornsay Colliery, 1900s. The old shaft could be the one that was located at the foot of West Street Gardens. It was possibly an exploration shaft because it was never used. The village was founded with the sinking of the colliery in 1868. It took its name from the nearby Old Cornsay, which was first mentioned in about 1183, when it was known as Corneshow.

Cornsay Colliery lodge banner, which shows a ship in troubled waters. The lodge was founded in 1889. The picture was taken in the village on the morning of a Durham Miners' Gala, 1900s.

ND - #0357 - 270225 - C0 - 276/195/15 - PB - 9781780913438 - Gloss Lamination